THE STORY OF THEODOR HERZL

(1860-1904)

RONNEN

The Story of

THEODOR HERZL

A Biography for Young People

by

ARTHUR SAUL SUPER

LONDON
VALLENTINE · MITCHELL

Published by
VALLENTINE, MITCHELL & CO., LTD.
37, Furnival Street, London, E.C.4.

Made and printed in Great Britain
by C. Tinling & Co. Ltd.
Liverpool, London and Prescot

Contents

For Stacia, with love

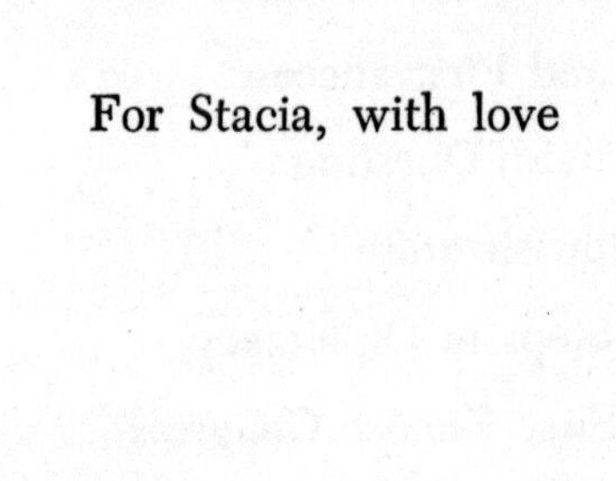

CHAPTER ONE

The Young Theodor

IT was always exciting when Grandpa came from Semlin, near Belgrade, to Pest, in Hungary, on one of his regular holiday visits. The old man would sit comfortably before the stove in the large living-room and ramble on for hours about his father and his grandfather, telling family legends that took you right back into the seventeenth century.

On such occasions young Theodor and his sister, Pauline, would sit at the large round table as quiet as mice. Sometimes they would play with the heavy woollen fringe of the thick reddish tablecloth that hung over the edges or tickled their knees, but usually they were all attention. There was so much to hear. Was it really true that long, long ago one of Father's ancestors had been stolen from his family in Spain and forced to become a Christian monk? And how exciting to learn that having been sent on a mission to a foreign land, he had escaped to Turkey and had returned to Judaism!

Some mornings, when Theodor came down earlier

than usual, he saw his grandfather standing erect and proud before the stove, winding leather straps around his bare forearm. He was wrapped in a prayer-shawl and a large skull-cap was pushed to the back of his head. He closed his eyes and fastened a leather box to his head while he quietly intoned a blessing. Theodor knew what his grandfather was doing because he had explained it all to him; but it fascinated him every time he saw it.

He listened to good-tempered arguments between his father, Jacob, and his grandfather, Simon Loeb Herzl. They covered the whole of Jewish life and customs. Simon Loeb was an interesting character. Although his two brothers had been converted to Christianity, he had clung devotedly to Judaism and observed all its prescriptions in his home town of Semlin, where the Herzl family had lived since the eighteenth century.

As they sat listening to their grandfather, Theodor and Pauline learned that before then the family had lived in Turkey. In 1712 the Herzls had moved to Belgrade, and only in 1737 had they settled in Semlin, which in those days was under the Austrian monarchy.

One of the things the old man talked about was the necessity for all Jews to return to their ancient homeland, Palestine. He seemed very excited over the theories of his local rabbi, Yehuda Hai Alkalai. Terrible things were happening in the Balkans. That was a mysterious place that seemed to involve revolutions, conspiracies, raids, murders, vendettas and feuds. Jews in the Balkan countries suffered a great deal. It was very difficult for them to carry on business; they were turned out of their homes, frequently at a moment's notice. They were often attacked and beaten; and even grimmer stories were told of people being killed in the streets.

Papa was always cold and scornful when the subject of Palestine came up. Why shouldn't the Jews fight for their place in the European society in which they lived? 'Look at my own case,' explained Jacob. 'I am doing quite well in the Bank of Hungary. I'm a director. The children lack nothing. Why all this hysterical nonsense?'

'That's just where you are wrong,' Grandfather would reply with a look of cunning triumph on his wrinkled old face. 'Reb Alkalai shows you it's not nonsense. He wants us Jews to form a joint stock company like a great commercial trust–a railway or something of that sort. A company would persuade the Sultan of Turkey to let the Jews have Palestine. Then they could organise a settlement company, sell land and develop into a small nation.'

'Please, Father,' Jacob would protest, 'don't quote that crazy Hebrew teacher and synagogue cantor at me. Business always looks easy to these amateurs. But it just wouldn't work.'

Theodor listened but kept very quiet, for if he asked questions he would be packed off to bed at once. But much of what he heard stuck in his memory.

Theodor was a strong, healthy boy with broad

shoulders and a sturdy frame which suggested he would be tall when grown up. He was handsome with large, dark, liquid eyes, a noble brow and a prominent chin. He had gentle good looks which he inherited from his mother.

Her family, the Diamants, had been in business in Pest for several generations and were reasonably well off. She was a beautiful woman with deep-set, brown eyes, dreamy yet fascinating. Sometimes, when she talked of her forebears, she would mention the great-great-grandfather who had died broken-hearted in a prison into which he had been thrown through anti-Jewish agitation.

She spent much of her time with Theodor and Pauline. She brought them up to be well-read and well-bred children, and introduced them to the culture of the German world, reading poems and stories to them.

She always called the boy Theodor, the German form of his name. The Hungarian form, which his playmates used, was Tivador; his Hebrew name was Benjamin Zev. Both she and his father lavished love and care on him. In those days children would go to school at the age of five, but Theodor was taught privately, so that he could be kept a little longer away from the rough and tumble of the ordinary school. His tutor was a kindly man and took to the boy, whom he later described as 'strong and lively,' a lad who behaved himself and learned quickly and well.

On May 2, 1866, Theodor was six years old. Now

he had to go to school and he became a pupil at the Jewish High School in Pest. Later, he remembered it was a strange sort of place. Looking back, he realised that his master had been a snob and had favoured him because his father was one of the rich parents. Theodor did not like this special treatment. Indeed, there was not much he did like about the school. The masters were mostly cold, unimaginative and dull. They seemed to resent having to teach the Bible, and other Jewish subjects, and the pupils realised it. One day, this got Theodor into trouble.

He had been reading the Bible at home and was enthralled with the Book of Exodus, especially the story of the departure from Egypt. It had everything to hold an imaginative boy: the great duel between Moses and Pharaoh, the plagues, the sense of doom of the last days of the bondage; the escape at midnight, the frantic flight of the 600,000 Hebrews towards the Red Sea; the pursuit by the Egyptian Army, the crossing on the dry sea-bed; the Egyptians trapped in the onrushing waters, and the Hebrew songs and dances of triumph as they came through safely to the farther shore.

So when the teacher announced that the Exodus would be the next day's lesson, Theodor was highly excited. But the teacher told the story in a dry, uninteresting fashion, as though it were a very unimportant historical event. He gave no hint that it was one of the most dramatic turning points in the history of the world. Theodor was disillusioned. 'Perhaps,' he thought, 'I'm taking it too literally. But the master ought to know. I won't bother about those Biblical fairy-tales any more.'

After that, he paid very little attention to his Jewish and Bible studies. Besides, many new and exciting things were happening just then. Why brood over miracles that might never have happened? Why worry about Jewish subjects when even the school-teachers seemed to think they were included in the syllabus simply to please the leaders of the Jewish community? And in any case, even they were more anxious for the children to be good at the ordinary subjects so as to keep up with the best schools in the city.

So instead of learning his lessons, Theodor spent his time reading everything he could get hold of about steam-engines, science, machinery and great achievements like the building of the Suez Canal that every-one was talking about.

But soon he had to pay for his neglect. It happened one bright morning when Theodor was sitting at his desk, drawing a sketch of a canal on his slate and mentally planning the great waterway he was going to cut between the two halves of the American continent, so that the waters of the Pacific Ocean would join those of the Atlantic. In his thoughts he was far away.

'Herzl,' the master shouted angrily. Theodor sat up with a start. 'You might tear yourself away from your important private concerns and repeat to your class-mates the story of the Exodus from Egypt,' he heard the teacher's sharp, sarcastic voice.

Theodor was confused. He could not remember one word. He stood red-faced and stammering. In the end, he stammered, 'I forget.'

'Then I have something to stimulate your memory,' the master cried. 'Come out here.'

By the time the boy reached the front of the class, the master had the cane in his hand, and had bared his arm to the elbow. He thrashed the backward pupil unmercifully.

This incident brought about an important change in Herzl's life. From early childhood he was not the sort of boy to be daunted by opposition or force. It seemed to stimulate him. But now it did not encourage him to improve his lessons. On the contrary, he paid no more attention to the school and the masters and began to concentrate on the subjects he liked best.

As he limped home with aching back and sore buttocks that afternoon he made his decision. He would be an engineer. That meant he would leave the stupid High School and go to the Technical School. Father would probably welcome that. He always defended modern existence against Grandfather, who loved the old world and the old ways. He passed the Reform synagogue which the family attended on Festivals and occasional Sabbaths, and craned his neck to look up at the two lofty towers which crowned the building, puzzled as always by the strange effect Moorish architecture had on a modern city. 'I'm through with you,' a voice inside him seemed to say as he turned into the gateway of his home, which was only a few steps from the synagogue.

If anything, Theodor's father was pleased with the decision. It was not too early for the boy to know what he wanted to do with his life. After all, he was ten years old.

As Jacob Herzl, tall and dignified in his top hat and long frock-coat, walked through the streets of Pest to the Technical School he had optimistic dreams for Theodor's future. 'We've done our best for the lad so far,' Jacob was thinking. 'His mother has given him an understanding of poetry, music and knowledge of the German cultural world. That will be useful to him, for he must know German to succeed as an engineer. And he seems to have a bent for it. He's always telling me how he will build this or erect that. Maybe some day. . . .'

The interview between Jacob Herzl and the headmaster was a little disappointing. He did not seem to share the father's enthusiasm over his son.

'We'll take the boy,' he said. 'But don't be so sure that he really has a talent for engineering. It's quite easy to make a mistake at his age. Most boys today are intensely aware of the new mechanical world and want to be engineers. But few have a vocation for it.'

'My dear Doctor,' Jacob answered, 'I do not think I'm mistaken. Theodor is always reading everything he can lay hands on about science and engineering.'

'Reading, Mr. Herzl, is one thing. But doing is

another. Is the boy always trying to make things with his hands?'

'Not more than most boys. But is that significant?'

'It might be or it might not,' the headmaster hedged. He went off on another tack. 'There are not many Jewish boys in this school, Mr. Herzl. Are you sure he will find his place here?'

'I see no reason why not. Theodor is a pleasant and sociable lad.'

'Well, we'll take him.'

And so, at the age of ten, Theodor became a student at the Pest City Technical School. The following years were crowded and not altogether happy. The headmaster proved to be right and Jacob Herzl wrong in their estimates of Theodor's abilities. It turned out that Theodor was not really interested in the machines but in what they could do to men and what men could do with them. He did not make great progress in the studies which were to fit him to be an engineer.

The years from ten to fourteen were a difficult period for Theodor. He was more sensitive than most children of his age. He came under many influences which drove his thoughts in different directions. He soon realised that engineering was not really his line, and the other boys were not very friendly. A new spirit was abroad in Hungary. The people were dissatisfied with Austrian rule and patriots were agitating for the liberation of the Hungarian people. Many of these were not content to try to unite the people against the Austrian rulers by stressing their Hungarian origins and viewpoint. Experience had taught them that one of the easiest ways to achieve unity was to influence and inflame the people against the Jews. Antisemitism began to grow among the Hungarians, especially in the city of Pest.

One of the causes of antisemitism is economic rivalry. This usually occurs at times of general depression, for it is then that antisemitism consoles those who have failed in business or suffered hardship, by suggesting it is not their fault or that of the Government. They can pretend they are in trouble because of unfair or dishonest Jewish competition. These lies are readily accepted, for no one likes to blame himself if he can find a scapegoat. The fact that the Jews also suffered in the general hardship did not count with the Hungarians, though in fact many Jews suffered even more, since at such times the Jewish employee was the first to be dismissed.

All this affected Theodor. At school the boys were quick to take it out of him, for their ideas had been picked up from their parents' talk at home.

On the whole the masters were hostile and unkind to the Jewish pupils. There was one in particular who made slighting references to Herzl's Jewishness which the sensitive boy received with a calm dignity that only served further to infuriate the master. In the class there was one boy, too, who constantly followed Herzl making loud remarks about 'that swarthy, skinny, Jew-boy.' Herzl took no notice and did not even look at his tormentor, but one day he turned on him with such rage in his eyes that the boy fled, and thereafter left Theodor alone. Perhaps it was at that moment that Herzl first subconsciously realised that the only final effective answer to anti-semitism was to build up anew the ancient dignity of the Jewish people.

The atmosphere at school affected Theodor's studies. He was not very interested in them in any case and now he did not bother to work. He was not helped by the fact that his father had business worries and ruin seemed to be not far away.

As his barmitzvah, his thirteenth birthday, approached, Theodor again grew intensely interested in Jewish thoughts and ideas. In preparation for this important event in his life, he began once more to study the Bible, the legends of his people and the main principles of his faith, from which he had turned when he was a small boy. They fascinated him. He dreamed about the Messiah who would come to redeem mankind. Possibly he even identified himself to some extent with that mythical figure. As he related in his diary later on, he told friends he had actually dreamt one night that the King Messiah came, bore him up upon a cloud, took him in his arms and showed him to Moses the Lawgiver, saying that this was the boy for whom he had been waiting. The Messiah then told Theodor to spread the message to the Jews.

Just about then old Rabbi Alkalai passed through the city which was now called Budapest. He had failed to make much of a stir in the Jewish world with his ideas about buying Palestine from the Sultan. But he himself in his old age was intending to settle in the Holy Land and from there to try to get some support. He paid a visit to the Herzls, and Theodor once more listened to his arguments and his father's objections. The great experience of his barmitzvah, with all the fuss, ceremony and solemnity of the occasion in the synagogue and at home, was behind him. He was better prepared to absorb some of Alkalai's ideas. He was old enough to know that not even his father was an infallible authority on business, although he still respected his opinions. And so a living spark of Alkalai's ideas remained somewhere deep in his mind and he now believed that he, Theodor Herzl, had something special to do in connection with those ideas.

However, like all normal, healthy boys, he lived in the present and the flush of day-to-day enthusiasm. He grew more and more backward in his studies and gained only a 'pass' at the end of the summer term of his fourteenth year, only just scraping through his final examinations.

If Theodor was a bad student, he found many other ways of displaying his capacities. He was the type of boy who would not easily take second place or live a life of little importance among his fellows. He was upset and unhappy about the ideas attending the revival of Hungarian nationalism. If the boys had not been so unfriendly and the leaders of the new Magyar movement so antisemitic, he might have directed all his energies and gifts into supporting it. But he turned his back on it. He turned to reading and scribbling. He organised a literary and debating society at school, and insisted that everyone kept to the rules he drew up. At the age of thirteen he had already learnt a very important truth: people must insist on a well-planned organisation and must stick to that organisation if they wanted to act together to achieve anything. People could share the same ideas, want the same things, but they would make no progress towards realising them unless they were organised. That meant putting down thoughts in black and white; reducing them to words and things which one could see and touch. And it also meant uniting people in a regular, disciplined body to carry out what was proposed.

But none of this activity helped Theodor at the Technical School. There was keen competition for places there and it was obvious that he did not fit in. By the time he was fifteen, his father had to admit that his son was not going to be an engineer who would rebuild the modern world. He took him away and sent him to the High School, where he could indulge his taste for literature.

Theodor had a full life at the High School. He liked his studies. He was a tall, handsome, impressive-looking youth. About this time he fell deeply in love with a girl slightly younger than himself. But he was not the sort to put all his energies into a boy-and-girl romance. He kept the image of Madeline, his youthful love, in his heart all his life. But nothing came of it, for life was urging him on to very serious matters.

Perhaps if they had met again after he had completed his studies it might have been different; but Madeline died young.

At the High School, Theodor found his place. Most of the pupils were Jewish so he was able to forget the antisemitism from which he had begun to suffer at the Technical School. His talent for organisation had a wider field in which to develop and flourish. It was a happy time in his life. For it was at this school that he began to write; poems, dramas, stories, articles. He started novels but did not finish them. There was almost no branch of literature which he did not try. On the surface he seemed completely carried away by the enthusiasm of the moment, but he was beginning to ponder the meaning of life very seriously.

Then suddenly it was as if a dark cloud covered the sky. His sister, Pauline, caught typhoid fever and died. The blow shattered the small, closely united Herzl family. To Theodor it seemed as if the end of the world had come. He and Pauline had been almost as one person. That slim, beautiful, lively girl had filled his heart with loving admiration. Through his mind ran pictures of their brief years together, especially of the miniature theatre which they had operated; he scribbling the plays as fast as he could write them, and Pauline acting them with real talent. With her bright flashing eyes, her long plaits, her expressive and melodious voice, she had been the most vivid person in his life. How they had fought and wrangled over the lines, the gestures, the production, and how their eyes had filled with tears of pride and achievement when they had put on one of their performances for an admiring circle of relatives and friends!

Pauline had just gone on from these childish games to success in her first professional appearance on the stage. Theodor had been inspired. In his youthful fancy, Pauline was to some extent his creation. He would have visions of writing plays for her that would bring world fame to both of them.

Now Pauline was dead and Theodor would never be completely happy again. For him and for his father and mother the familiar scenes of Budapest could no longer be endured. They moved to Vienna where Theodor, now eighteen years old, entered the university to study law, or so his father thought. However, at this period he knew what he wanted to do more than anything else. That was to be a writer and live by selling his ideas to people who would gladly pay to hear what the brilliant young Theodor Herzl had to tell them.

CHAPTER TWO

Awakening in Vienna

VIENNA in 1878. The capital of an empire curiously compounded of Eastern and Western civilisations. A city of light and music and gaiety and an exciting beauty; a centre of literature and art, of conflict and debate without end.

For Theodor Herzl, this was the very centre of the world he was eager to conquer. His parents wanted him to study law; well, he would study law; but that could not prevent him from writing.

It was Rabbi Kohn who finally forced the decision shortly before the family had actually left Budapest. Theodor felt that with his mother's help he might have been permitted to give himself entirely to literature. She had prepared him for it by her readings, by her own exquisite taste, by her passionate interest in all that was new and alive in the German artistic revival of the second half of the nineteenth century.

But Rabbi Kohn, serious, cautious and sagacious, had struck a responsive chord in Jacob Herzl's heart.

Theodor's father had begun to climb slowly out of the morass of his serious business reverse and was winning his way to a respectable, middle-class competence. He recognised that his son had many of the attributes of genius. But this very fact made him afraid that he might become a Bohemian if he did not have the discipline of a long, intensive course of study for a profession.

'Ah, my dear Herzl,' Kohn had said. 'A writer. What is he? The envy of many. Many doors open to him. He might write a successful play and the bright light of fame may shine upon him for a while. But what is he in truth? An entertainer. Not much more. But does he enjoy real respect? A young man needs a solid basis of training, a profession.'

But only part of Theodor's mind was given to his studies. There was so much to see, hear and do. There were so many young men like himself, with ideas to challenge his own. And always there was the world of journalism, literature and drama, only waiting to be conquered.

Rabbi Kohn was sound, sensible and safe, but how could he be expected to realise the thrill of seeing one's own words printed in a newspaper? What could Rabbi Kohn know of the thrill of hearing your own words, the product of your imagination, spoken by actors on the stage? All he knew about was how to preach sober, careful words each week to his congregation in the synagogue.

Herzl's words would arouse tears and joy, laughter and sorrow, in the hearts of thousands of men and women. And because he had written for them his emotions would become their emotions, his thoughts their thoughts. He never wavered in this belief that he would conquer the world of the theatre, despite the fits of depression which attacked him during those student years as the rejection slips piled up. Once, when he was out walking with a great friend, Arthur Schnitzler, along the broad avenues of Vienna, they passed the Burg Theatre, the centre of longing of every aspiring playwright in Austria. Herzl looked at the playbills outside.

'One day soon, one of my plays will be produced there.' But that was still in the future. In the meantime he had to attend lectures and study. He joined the Akademische Lesehalle, the university debating society, an association of over a thousand students, with a membership unrestricted by creed, class or politics. Here every subject under the sun was debated in an atmosphere of complete equality and freedom. It seemed the right organisation for him to join. He knew he was a Jew, but he felt that this did not make him conspicuously different from any other Austrian. However, in those days no sensitive person could ignore the fact that the Jew in Austria had some difficulty in fitting into and being accepted by his environment. That Theodor was aware of this can be deduced from the plays he was writing. But the Debating Society had a reputation for tolerance. One of its most distinguished presidents was a Jewish lawyer, Dr. Alfred Bachrach, who said: 'In the shrine of knowledge, all who come to worship are equal.'

In this body the tall, handsome young man soon made his mark. He became responsible for its literary activities, but, surprisingly enough, did not take much part in public debate. He was more content to listen and register impressions. Occasionally he might make a witty interjection or shrewd comment, deflating some too high-flown idea. Jewish questions came up now and then, but Herzl expressed no definite opinions and did not get involved. At times he showed unmistakably that he was irritated by the excessive enthusiasm of some of his fellow-Jewish students for current movements and ideas. He did not realise that this discomfort was the first, clear sign of his special sensitivity to the Jewish question.

In Austria nationalism was a growing force; so was antisemitism. In theory the Jews were equal before the law. In fact they had to suffer many restrictions. No Jew could hope to become a professor. No Jewish doctor could look forward to an appointment in a leading hospital, and no Jewish lawyer could expect to get to the top of his profession. Herzl knew this, and it worried him. But, like the other Jews of his time, he persuaded himself that all these obstacles to full Jewish freedom would disappear as people became accustomed to Jewish emancipation.

They did not disappear. The echoes of the strife and conflict in the world outside penetrated into the university. The struggle for Austrian nationalism, the clashes between liberals and reactionaries in politics, were increasingly reflected in debates and hot arguments inside the Debating Society. One of the main issues was antisemitism. Because Jews felt that their problems would vanish as men grew more liberal, many of them associated themselves with the Liberal Party. As a result the opponents of the Liberals tried to get the people to identify them with the Jews. They knew that there was always a traditional latent hatred of the Jew. It was a disease which had eaten into the hearts of men for centuries. So they deliberately fomented this hatred in order to discredit their opponents.

Thus a new form of antisemitism began to spread in Vienna. It soon infected the Debating Society, and after a rowdy meeting harangued by an antisemitic agitator, the police closed it down.

Herzl still believed that this agitation would pass. He became a member of the student fraternity called Albia. It had only a few Jewish members. He found it very exciting to bustle around the city and university in his pill-box cap, wearing his badge and the gold, blue, and white ribbon of membership on his student uniform. He liked the thrills of the students' duels. He took lessons from a fencing master, and one day he had to face his first fight. His opponent was from the Allemania, or German Society. They fought fiercely. Herzl wounded his man, but himself received a deep cut which required stitching. He had acquitted himself well. Two further challenges came to nothing because his opponents apologised and withdrew.

He liked the merry drinking, shouting, joking and laughter which followed such encounters, and he plunged eagerly into this life. He was very popular. The sketches he wrote caused guffaws of laughter, and writing them came easily to him. He took this as a sign that he would soon succeed in writing for the commercial theatre and the newspapers. He had a quantity of work in hand, but he was too frequently distracted by the card games, the beer parties, the rambles, the singing sessions, the fencing lessons that were part of life in the Albia.

Yet while he entered into these activities with all the zest of his passionate nature, he was not completely satisfied. He had to study, but this did not disturb him unduly. He did not succeed in his writing because what he produced was too close a reflection of his personal and social life. The characters he drew were shallow and unreal. They said the sort of witty things that students loved to hear, but did not appear as round human beings.

'My boy,' he said one day to his bosom friend, Staerk, 'I'm getting fed up with all this playing around.' 'Why, Theo,' his friend replied, 'you're doing fairly well. You passed your first exams with distinction.'

'I don't know. I suppose all of us sons of rich parents feel we can afford to fool around and have a good time at the university. But have we no responsibilities to others? There must be more than that in life. And this should be where we find out what we have to do.'

One of the reasons for Herzl's restlessness was the greater degree to which the new antisemitic theories were beginning to affect the life of the students. They were infecting the Albia, whose members were supposed to be his brothers-in-arms and comrades.

For example, there was Ritter von Schoenerer. He often spoke at student meetings. It was this man whose vile antisemitic tirades at the Debating Society had led to the police raid and its closing down.

Then he had had less support, now there were far too many students who openly declared that they agreed with him. Herzl often attacked such students vigorously, but they either contemptuously ignored his remarks or reacted with open hostility. The climax came when a leading member of Albia, Hermann Bahr, spoke on the composer Wagner's antisemitism. The audience expressed its approval. Violent arguments broke out, chairs were thrown, heads were broken, and the police arrived.

Herzl was not present at the meeting, but he could not let the incident pass unnoticed. He waited a few days, hoping the Albia would issue some public statement disowning Bahr's views. Nothing happened.

'This is more than I can stand,' Herzl said. 'I no longer feel comfortable in this society.'

'Why?' his friend said. 'You're a member. No one has said anything to you. It will pass over.'

'I don't think so,' Herzl answered. 'Do you think I'd be accepted if I applied for membership now? I am a Jew, and the Albia has, by implication, endorsed all the vile libels about Jews circulated by Richard Wagner and Duhring.'

'It will pass over,' came the reply.

'No. It won't. I shall resign. I shall write and tell them so.'

The friend left and Herzl sat down in fury and wrote a letter which showed up with deadly logic the immoral course the Albia was taking. The committee of the Albia was equally furious when they read it. 'Why should we let him resign?' the President sneered. 'We'll expel him. The impertinence of this fellow, writing to us like that!'

However, this disgrace was averted. When a number of the members heard of the committee's proposal they refused to endorse it. Herzl was allowed to resign quietly.

The way in which the feeling against the Jews was being fanned into a new and dangerous form of anti-semitism had long disturbed him. He had for some time believed that the nineteenth century was at last witnessing the end of the anti-Jewish feeling which had reduced Jewry to misery, destitution and degradation through the ages. He had often heard the subject discussed in his home. Now scraps of those conversations returned to his mind.

'Everything is different now,' his father would say. 'Since the French Revolution the world has learned that all men are equal. We Jews are now the same as any other people. We have a different religion, that is all. But otherwise I'm as good as an Austrian or a Hungarian or anyone you care to mention. I go to synagogue and worship my God in the Jewish fashion. Otherwise there is nothing to mark me off from the butcher, the baker or candlestick-maker around the corner, or the colonel in the garrison or the professor at the University.'

'That's the situation exactly,' his mother would add. 'You must recall what was said in Napoleon's time: "For Jews as a people nothing, for Jews as a religion only everything."'

And only now did Herzl feel that he knew what the argument was about. His parents roundly asserted that Jews were exactly the same as everyone else except for their religion. But to his eye they looked very different. There was old Rabbi Alkalai for one, with his impressive beard, his strange tricks of speech, his interesting fund of curious knowledge, his wonderful theories about a Jewish homeland. There was his grandfather and the customs he observed and the ritual of his daily life. There were the Jewish beggars in the streets and the frightening stories they told of pogroms, butchery and expulsions, of flights in terror from one inhospitable land to another.

At home he was told that it was his sufferings that had warped the Jew, turning him sometimes into a cunning, shrewd character bent on survival at any price and providing for his family by any means, however shady. 'Many Christian thinkers of today are saying quite plainly that if some Jews are out of tune with the modern world it is because of the treatment they received at the hands of Gentiles,' his mother asserted.

But Herzl also remembered hearing Rabbi Alkalai once say:

'Our good Christian friends, who so generously

apologise for us today, are ignorant of the fact or forget that we Jews had schools and our great academies of learning at a time when Europe was primitive and illiterate, and we saw to it that every boy, and some girls too, could read and write. We had a rich inner spiritual life they knew nothing about and which all they did to us could not destroy or damage.'

All these conversations had combined to give Herzl the impression that an increasing liberalism would finally solve the Jewish problem. He read extensively during his college years, Byron, Voltaire, Macaulay and Balzac, and the German philosophers and historians. He fed his romantic imagination on Henri Murger's scenes of Bohemian life, with its description of artists and writers living, laughing and weeping, but also creating under the rooftops of Paris. He dipped into the heavy, turgid Russian novelists. And all the time he was writing, writing, writing.

The parting with the Albia had been preordained. Herzl must have sensed that when he came across Eugen Duhring's work on the Jewish question. He expressed hatred; naked, dirty, unscrupulous and venomous. Duhring completely rejected any theories that time would solve the Jewish question. Nothing Jews could do or become would ever make them acceptable. There was some racial trait in them, in their very blood, which was ineradicably vile; an hereditary evil of permanent menace to the whole world.

Herzl was shocked to his depths, and he flatly rejected Duhring's thesis. He still believed that time would cure the world of its wrong attitude towards Jews. He said:

'These childish fables will vanish. In the new world which is dawning mankind will look at the problem calmly and without prejudice. It will see its own past errors in the same perspective as educated men today look back on the murky darkness of the Middle Ages.'

Yet in spite of this optimistic view which he had expressed less than two years previously, in 1883 Herzl had to admit that Duhring's ideas were gaining ground and had won the agreement of many intellectuals.

The last year of his university career was devoted to completing his studies as creditably as possible, but he found time to write more dramas, more essays and more articles. In some of these the conflicts in his own mind over the Jewish question are faithfully mirrored in the words he put into the mouths of his characters. In the essays he escaped from his troubles into the world of creative writing about interesting aspects of life. He was beginning to be published; editors were slowly awakening to the fact that a new and noble talent was developing in their midst.

He was lonely, but his father gave him money to travel and he spent his vacations taking long and interesting rambles through Europe. In 1883 he toured through Austria, Hungary and Switzerland. In 1884, he graduated as a Doctor of Laws and went off on an extended visit to Paris, the world centre of the arts, literature and his beloved theatre.

CHAPTER THREE

Love and First Success

THEODOR HERZL was just over 24 years of age when, in August 1884, he accepted a post as a law officer in the service of the State. He spent some months learning the routine of work in the Government Legal Department, and almost a year later he was attached to the Civil Court at Salzburg.

Life was not too dull for the young Government lawyer. His mornings and early afternoons were spent in his office. There were documents to look up and study, briefs to write, reports to make and innumerable forms to be filled in. His heart was not in his work, but he was conscientious, and impressed the mark of a fine intellect even on the dry legal procedures. His superiors praised him highly.

But it was a different Herzl who closed the door on the musty files, and went out into the clear fresh air. He read everything he could. He was often very melancholy. Once he said: 'There is no such thing as youth. It's just a figment of the imagination. What are the joys of youth? They don't exist. Old men have made up fairy tales about it in order to fool themselves that once they were happy and strong and free.'

Theodor had often suffered from similar attacks of depression. While still a student, at the age of 22, he had been depressed at not winning a prize offered by the 'Neue Freie Presse' of Vienna. 'Better,' he wrote in his diary, 'to wipe my lips and leave the job of writing many books to others. That would be the best, wisest and most honest thing for me to do after this proof that I have no talent.'

On another occasion he wrote: 'I can now say that I shall never be reckoned among the men who make a mark on their generation. . . . I am 22 and what have I done? Nothing.'

A year later he told himself: 'There is no love in my heart, no aspiration in my soul. No hopes, no joys . . . everything empty . . . heart empty of hope, mind empty of thoughts, pockets empty of cash and life empty of poetry. . . .'

The picture was not all that bad. He seems to have fallen in and out of love more than once, but these were not serious attachments. All in all, life was not too unbearable. The dull routine by which he earned his bread only gave him more zest for life and more intensity in living every moment of his day, the glad times as well as the sad. It was while he was at Salzburg that he finally decided to give up law and devote himself entirely to writing. It was a wise decision. He was a born journalist and writer. Later he was to attain immortality as the great leader of the Jewish people, but in the meantime he wrote about 30 plays, some of which achieved success in the theatres of many lands. He published several books of essays, and many of them are still remembered and quoted by men who appreciate superlative work in the field of literature.

Herzl resigned from the Legal Department on August 5, 1885, and began to travel through Europe. He supported himself by all sorts of hack writing, but was encouraged by a report that one of his plays had succeeded in New York. He also wrote a weekly column for the 'Berliner Tageblatt', one of the great newspapers of his time. His reputation was growing steadily and on April 1, 1887, when he came back from his tour of Europe, he was appointed features editor of the 'Wiener Allgemeine Zeitung'. It was a post of great distinction. At the age of 27 Herzl could claim to be a journalist of recognised international standing. Moreover, he had several plays waiting to be produced or finished and the prospects were good.

One day, on May 14, 1887, he stood in his office thinking over his life.

'Here I am,' he told himself, 'a great success. I have arrived as a journalist, but otherwise I'm finished.'

He sighed deeply, and thought again with pain and longing of his blonde, blue-eyed Julie. It was fifteen months since he had stood on the balcony with the lovely, provocative, 18-year-old youngest daughter of the great industrialist, Joseph Naschauer, and had stolen his first kiss from her. She had turned away and blushed when he asked for the kiss, and had said:

'No, darling, you will tell people.'

'I'd die rather than do that,' he whispered fervently; and she had turned and pressed her soft lips to his. As they opened the french windows and stepped back into the room, his spirit cried gladly: 'It's unbelievable, impossible, but true. I'm in love.'

Memories of their love passed with a bitter-sweet pain through Herzl's mind. There was the time, a month after that first kiss, when they stood clasped in each other's arms exchanging kisses on the balcony of Julie's house while only two paces away, in the room, her irascible father sat with a couple of cronies. It was the thought of her father that made Herzl feel he could not go on like this. He had made Julie fall in love with him and he was in love with her. But he was so much older than she—eight years. He was mature enough to know that it could never work out well. What had he to offer this millionaire's daughter? A modest competence as the wife of a writer. She was used to furs, jewels, carriages, spacious drawing-rooms, dazzling company, servants to wait on her, and a social whirl and lavish hospitality to which he could never aspire.

His mother, too, was against the romance which she could see developing. But it was doubtful if his mother would have welcomed any daughter-in-law, for she was completely wrapped up in her son and was loth to share him with any woman. Herzl reciprocated his mother's feeling, and his deepest love was always to be for his mother. He did not fully realise the reason, but he felt that there were almost insuperable problems on both sides.

He recalled how he had tried to quarrel with Julie so that she should cease to love him. On a fine evening in May, he and she had been together, snatching furtive kisses on the balcony and behind the pillars. They had met to talk over what her father had said to him as he left the house the previous evening:

'I have told my daughter,' Naschauer had said coldly, 'that you will never be allowed to marry her. Don't waste your time courting her. This affair has no future. She is a child of 18, you are 26 and a man of the world. What can she expect to gain from it?'

He also learned from this conversation that Julie had defied her father and told him that she loved Theodor.

Theodor made up his mind that he would have to make the sacrifice and 'cure' her of her love for him. He would neglect her, make her feel unhappy, and then she would no longer care for him so passionately. But meantime they stood on the balcony and kissed each other, and he thought they would never be so close again. So far as he could see, this was good-bye.

Ten days later, Julie told him that she and the family would be at the Burg Theatre. He did not go to the theatre but sat waiting at the café opposite, so that she should see him and know that he was slighting her deliberately. Julie acknowledged him with a nod when he formally greeted her as her carriage drew up outside the theatre. At eleven o'clock he went to the hotel where she was sitting with her family at supper, sat down with them, and deliberately talked to everyone but her. He saw her eyes darken and cloud with pain, and sorrow filled his heart. When the party broke up she did not say one word. She only nodded to him, but her look told him all she felt.

But it was all no use. The next day they made it up and were more in love than ever. Herzl told her why he had been so foolish and cold and she smiled at him through her tears, saying simply:

'That way you will never make me cease to love you.'

They were hopelessly in love and something would have to be done. Meanwhile he had gone travelling through Europe, and now he had this offer which would bring him back to Vienna and an assured position. But it still did not justify his asking for Julie's hand.

In the next few months his reputation grew rapidly and at last he felt justified in becoming engaged to Julie. They announced their betrothal in 1887 and on July 25, 1889, were married at Reichenau and went off on an eight-week honeymoon, travelling in Switzerland and France. Meanwhile a house had been prepared for them in Vienna.

The marriage did not fulfil their high hopes of happiness. Herzl's fears were realised. The change from the great luxury of her father's home to the modest competence he was able to provide for her soon set Julie at odds with her husband. Herzl's mother did not take kindly to her new daughter-in-law and interfered with the young couple a good deal. Theodor never quite freed himself from his mother as the dominating feminine influence in his life. A daughter, Pauline, named after Herzl's beloved sister, was born on March 29, 1890, and a son, Hans, followed on June 10, 1891.

Herzl's delight in his children knew no bounds, but it could not save his marriage. Earlier that year his dearest friend had shot himself, and this plunged him into melancholy. His relations with Julie grew worse. The gay, carefree girl found the humdrum domestic round hard going with this moody, unhappy and tortured man who was so much older than herself. He in turn sought solitude in order to wrestle with his problems.

Two months after Hans was born, he set out alone on a journey through France and Spain. At St. Jean de Luz he found peace and contentment, and the article he wrote about it for the 'Neue Freie Presse', caused a literary sensation. In October 1890, the newspaper, one of the most influential and famous in Europe, cabled offering him the post of Paris correspondent with a handsome salary and allowances. In November Julie joined him in Paris and they patched up their marriage with a kind of reconciliation. It was still not what Julie wanted, but she tried to make the best of it. Later there was a third child of the marriage, Margaret (called Trude), who was born in May 1893. Whatever happiness came to Herzl was always overshadowed by the Jewish question, which now began to enter into the serious thoughts he had about life. He still thought time or some other simple remedy would solve it. He met with antisemitism occasionally, but only twice did he see it in something of its naked savagery, and even then it hardly affected him directly.

'I heard the cry "Hep, Hep!" only twice in my life,' he wrote in his diary in 1896. 'Once I was passing through the city of Mainz, in Germany, and I went into a cheap restaurant. That was in 1888. There seemed to be some sort of musical evening in progress. I ordered a glass of beer. I drank it down and got up to leave. As I made my way through the crowd, I heard a young fellow scream after me, "Hep, Hep!" and his sally was greeted by shouts of raucous and drunken laughter.'

'Hep, Hep!' is the shout which for centuries was raised by German mobs as they plundered and murdered Jews in the medieval ghettos. The word is supposed to consist of the initials of the Latin words *Hierosolyma est perdita* (Jerusalem is destroyed), which echoes the Roman exultation over the downfall of the second Jewish commonwealth in the year 70 C.E.. The shout did not trouble Herzl at that time, but it left its mark on him, for several years later, when he began his work to rebuild the Jewish State, he recalled and wrote down the incident.

The second time he heard a similar cry, Herzl wrote, was in Baden, a summer resort near Vienna. It was September 1893, and he was spending a month's vacation with his friend, Ludwig Spiedel. They had taken a long walk in the lovely Vienna woods. As the gentle influence of the carefully tended countryside brought peace to their hearts they discussed the Jewish problem.

'I understand this antisemitism,' said Herzl. 'We Jews have remained, through no fault of our own, a strange element in society. In the ghetto we inherited a number of characteristics which still make us unpopular. The things that happened to us warped us, but now we can correct this by bringing other things to pass which will have a contrary effect.'

'But the antisemitism we are witnessing now is a new thing,' Spiedel protested.

'Of course it is,' Theodor answered. 'It's the result of our emancipation. But the ignorant mob, who support antisemitism, do not see that we Jews are what they have made us by their vicious ill-treatment.'

'What do you mean?' said Spiedel.

'Well, take usury for example. We became moneylenders because the Church, throughout the ages, did not let us do anything else. So we began to love money too much. We had to have our possessions in the form of gold and jewels which we could take with us if we had to flee from any country.'

'There is something in that,' Spiedel said, 'but Jews were also agents and servants for the rulers, weren't they?'

'Yes. We did their dirty work. We squeezed money out of the people by means of loans and interest, or by farming taxes, and then the ruler squeezed us. So we became the hated instruments of indirect taxation.'

'Hardly calculated to make Jews very popular,' Spiedel suggested. 'No wonder there were so many pogroms and massacres.'

'Once we were a noble and proud people and knew how to defend ourselves. We had such qualities that 2,000 years of persecution have not destroyed them completely,' Herzl declared.

'And now the new liberalism should put things right, perhaps,' Spiedel added.

'I thought so for many years,' Herzl answered. 'I am not so sure now. You can't make men equal or reform them by a statute or a decree.'

The argument continued till they returned home, and went on late into the night.

'Then what is the answer?'

'Adaptation, Ludwig. Ever heard of Charles Darwin? He puts forward the theory that the species adapts itself. We shall do the same. By living with the Gentiles, by imitating their ways, by being forced into the political and economic currents and influences which determine their lives, we shall become like them. When that process is completed, we shall be free of the problem.'

'Here in our Fatherland,' Ludwig concluded.

'In our Austrian Fatherland,' assented Herzl.

When he was leaving Spiedel's house that night he heard some vicious hooligans shout 'Pig of a Jew' at him. He went white with anger. His first impulse was to run after them, but they had already made off. He calmed down almost immediately.

'It's not me personally they wish to insult,' he

told himself. 'They don't know me at all. It was my Jewish nose and my Jewish beard they were sneering at. So much for all my fine thoughts about time and liberalism solving this problem.'

CHAPTER FOUR

The Jewish Question

HERZL'S new post as Paris correspondent of the 'Neue Freie Presse' had a great influence on his future rôle. As the representative of one of the most important newspapers in Europe, he had to mingle with the great ones of the earth. He could meet them, if not on terms of equality, at least with much less diffidence that he might otherwise have felt. Moreover, his closeness to the great political and social issues of the day gave him a deep insight into and an understanding of statesmen, diplomats and politicians.

He settled in Paris at a time when the capital was being rocked by some of the most violent controversies of the age and, as a newspaperman, he was involved in them, even if only objectively. France was passing through crisis after crisis. She had endured many setbacks to her prestige and was anxious to find a scapegoat. Antisemites breed very quickly in such fertile ground, and France soon produced hers. Edouard Drumont obliged with a book entitled

'La France Juive' which was a more vicious attack on Jewry than anything Duhring had produced. It was readily accepted and won popularity even among the French intellectuals.

Herzl had a pretty shrewd idea what antisemitism meant to a ruling class which wanted to divert the people's minds from their real problems. In one of his articles he said: 'For many centuries Jews have been specially useful instruments, to be used by Governments to pretend that it is they, the Jews, who are responsible for all the misery and unhappiness, corruption and distortion practised on their people. There are elements in the Governments which will keep Jews alive simply so that they can perform this function.'

Herzl was now considering solution after solution to the Jewish question. He had covered for his paper the story of a certain antisemitic aristocrat, the Marquis de Mores, who had killed a Jewish staff officer, Captain Mayer, in a duel which he had provoked. 'That's a good idea,' he thought one day. 'I shall challenge one of the world's leading antisemites to a duel. I shall kill him. Then, when I'm brought up for trial, the eyes of all the world will be upon me. "Yes," I shall say. "I killed this antisemite." I shall prove that Jews are not afraid to defend themselves. To explain my act I shall bring the vileness of antisemitism out into the open.'

But that was only a dream, although the letter in which he set down these thoughts shows the way his mind was working.

About this time, he handled another story. There was a man named Paul Friedmann who sold all he had to finance a plan to rebuild a Jewish State in the land of Midian, a part of ancient Palestine. Friedmann's scheme was a failure. But it had one effect. The magic words 'Jewish State' passed through Herzl's mind.

The widow of the proprietor of the 'Neue Freie Presse' invited him to take part in a 'League Against Antisemitism' which she and some influential friends were organising.

'There's something laughable about this sort of thing,' Herzl said. 'It's like a relief committee after or before a flood. It doesn't prevent the flood and doesn't repair the ravages when it does come.'

A few years earlier Herzl had been favourable to the idea of founding a popular newspaper of wide circulation to defend the Jews and attack antisemitism. Now, in 1893, he felt sure it was a useless and even a foolish notion.

In this same year he thought up a great plan for the mass conversion of Jews. This would at least solve the problem as far as Austria was concerned, provided the Catholic Church could be brought to co-operate. His idea was to obtain an introduction to the Pope through the local Catholic Church dignitaries. Then, Herzl would say to him:

'Your Holiness, help us to quench the flood of antisemitism and I, for my part, will undertake to stir up a mighty movement among the Jews which will lead them voluntarily and without friction into Christianity.'

When the Pope inquired what Herzl meant by 'without friction', he would tell him: 'I myself, Your Holiness, and leading members of my generation, would remain Jews, and as such we would preach to the others the benefits of joining the dominant faith. Then in broad daylight, on one chosen Sunday, in the full blaze of noon, to the gay sound of pealing bells, the converts would march in festive procession to St. Stephen's. They would not walk in shame or embarrassment but with a proud step.'

'And what about the leaders who had persuaded them to do all this?' the Pope might ask.

'Oh, they would remain outside. The very fact that they remained Jews would prove the sincerity of the undertaking and that it was quite voluntary.'

As Herzl saw it, his generation would be the border generation, remaining in the faith of their fathers. But their children would be Christians, before they were old enough to decide for themselves.

He had the whole thing worked out in detail. He planned and foresaw his conversation with the Archbishop of Vienna and the Pope. He sought an opportunity to put the suggestion before his newspaper proprietor, for he felt that if he supported it, the idea would be much more readily accepted.

'Herr Benedikt,' he said, after explaining the plan, 'not only is it good in itself, it might have important implications in helping the Liberal Party which you support.'

Moritz Benedikt was not impressed. After arguing with Herzl and listening patiently to what he had to say, he said quietly:

'Dr. Herzl, for centuries your ancestors clung to Judaism. Are you really content to take the responsibility of ending the process? I say you cannot do so and you are unable to do it. In any case, the Pope will never receive you.'

'Well,' Herzl thought as he slowly walked home after the interview, 'if the paper doesn't support it, it's difficult to know where to begin to popularise the idea.'

He let the matter rest for a few weeks, but in the meantime his mind turned over the fundamentals of the Jewish question a thousand times. He studied historical instances of mass conversion. He was getting close to the true solution to the problem, and his new line of thought was not simply the result of eliminating other possibilities. He was beginning to realise that 'his' Jewish question, as he now called it, could only be resolved if the Jews had a State of their own where they could live as they liked, do as they liked and not be interfered with by others or suffer persecution; or be forced into unpleasant professions and trades, only to be blamed for the bad effects this treatment had upon their characters. He was beginning to see that it was useless for Jews to wander from land to land seeking peace and full acceptance by non-Jews. The antisemites would not stand Jews no matter what they did to conform. They might become Christians, they might make firm friends; they might help their fellow-men, be great philanthropists; it did not matter. A time of trial and crisis was bound to come, and then the Jew would find the man he thought his friend was a stranger or even an enemy. Then he would discover that he had been foolish to suppress his Judaism; to cast it aside in the hope of making peace with the antisemites. There could be no peace with that disease so long as the Jewish people were homeless. Give the Jews a home and you will have cured antisemitism. In curing antisemitism the way is also cleared for curing many of the general ills of society. For you deprive evil and wicked men of this weapon of antisemitism which they use to blind the unthinking and credulous masses to the real causes of their misfortunes.

One day, in October 1894, while he was sitting posing in the studio of a sculptor friend, Samuel Friedrich Beer, the two men talked. Herzl was 34 years of age, in the bloom of his early maturity. His beard was full, square and impressive, like that of Assyrian kings engraved on monuments. He had a fine moustache and his broad, noble brow indicated a keen intelligence; emphatic eyebrows shrouded the keen gaze of eyes which could shift very quickly from sternness to laughter and then cloud over in sudden melancholy.

He was pondering on the Jewish question. 'What happens,' he thought, 'when we Jews give up our love of money?' His answer was put into words: 'It won't help the Jews in the least even if they all become artists. We shall never leave the ghetto.'

He grew very excited. He broke off the sitting and rushed into the street. He had a new play in his head, his greatest. If only he did not have to slave for the paper he could write it in a couple of weeks. By the time he had walked a short way the whole plot was worked out in his mind. In two weeks he managed to complete the drama, which he called 'The New Ghetto'. It contained his basic thinking on the need for a Jewish State, but it was expressed in the form of a play dealing with the Jew in modern European society.

What had brought him to his clear realisation of the need for this Jewish State? The one event above all others was the trial of a Jew, Captain Dreyfus, which had begun in December 1894.

Dreyfus, an officer on the French General Staff, was accused of selling military secrets to a foreign Power. He was found guilty on what afterwards turned out to be completely fabricated evidence. The French military authorities publicly stripped him of his rank and sentenced him to 20 years' confinement on Devil's Island, the penal colony off the coast of South America. After some years, following a desperate struggle to obtain a new hearing, Dreyfus was cleared and restored to his rank.

In 1895, however, no one knew that Dreyfus was innocent, although some, including Herzl, were uneasy about the worth of the evidence produced to secure his conviction. Herzl was even more worried about the manner in which the trial was conducted and the atmosphere in which it was held. It seemed almost as though it was not Dreyfus who was being tried but the Jewish people. Angry, violent mobs surrounded the court and raged through the streets and public squares screaming, 'Death to the Jews!' The feeling inside the court was equally tense and foul. Herzl could not help noticing the glee with which all present, from the judge downwards, set about condemning the prisoner. The witnesses' testimony dripped with malice as they deliberately drew the rope round the neck of Dreyfus. The journalists in the press-box were rather uneasy about the whole business. Nevertheless, Herzl's immediate neighbour, not knowing he was a Jew, turned to him and said:

'What does it matter? He is only a Jew.'

The words echoed in Herzl's mind later when he stood in the square and saw the French soldiers drawn up to witness Captain Dreyfus's disgrace. His epaulettes were ripped from his shoulders and his sword was broken in two. Desperate, ashen-faced, but still dignified he stood and cried:

"I am innocent. *Vive la France!*'

It was the Dreyfus case which brought Herzl to his final views on the Jewish question. He considered many solutions to the problem of how a Jew can live in a world in which he is not allowed to or cannot find his place. Jews had to conform to the customs and the laws of the countries in which they lived. They could serve those countries in the most important positions. But that would not ensure their safety. The new antisemitism went beyond religious differences and was based on theories of race and blood. In the face of such fanaticism it was idle to hope that liberalism would solve anything. The supreme example of the failure of that solution had just been provided in France, the land of its birth, where the emancipation of the Jews had begun less than a century previously.

Shortly after the Dreyfus tragedy, Herzl was sitting with a friend at a small table in a Paris café, sipping coffee and brooding over the election of Karl Lueger, a notorious antisemite, as Mayor of Vienna.

'It's a terrible thing for Austria that such a man has been elected Burgomaster. What does it mean?' the friend asked Herzl anxiously.

'And this Dreyfus affair. That spells the betrayal of all the ideals of the French Revolution,' Herzl answered. He stared down at the dregs in his coffee cup. Suddenly his eyes lit up and he threw a humorous look at his friend:

'Why are you, the Parisian, so upset by Lueger's election and I, the Viennese, so disturbed by the Dreyfus affair, if you are only a Frenchman and I am only an Austrian?'

His friend looked up startled and perplexed, but Herzl's thoughts were far away.

'I have never been concerned about my Jewishness,' he told himself. 'But now I see where I have to go. I have always been close to the answer but I never grasped it till this minute. Strange that it was so close yet I never saw it!'

He went to the synagogue in the Rue de la

Victoire. The service with its Hebrew prayers, its nostalgic melodies, its imagery and poetry, made a deep impression on him. His mind went back to the Budapest Synagogue close to his childhood home. He looked searchingly at the faces of the Jews who were sitting there. Did he detect a general family resemblance in all of them? Did they all have prominent noses and a look of mingled fear and cunning in their eyes? If they had that look, it was Gentile persecution which had caused it. If they had their own State it would not matter how ugly or how handsome they looked.

The thought came into his mind that he would like to travel through the great centres of Jewish settlement, to Russia, Galicia, Hungary and Bohemia. He wanted to go and see the new Jewish colonies which some Jews were struggling to establish in Palestine. By seeing all these places with his own eyes and then coming back and comparing the Jews there with Western Jewry, he might be able to present a true picture of Jews as they really were, the victims of a tragedy.

In the spring of that year he had a talk with the famous French novelist, Daudet. The conversation turned to the Jewish question.

'You must know, Herzl,' the writer said quite coolly, 'that I am an antisemite.'

Herzl passionately explained his views on the Jewish question and said:

'I am thinking of writing a book about it.'

'A novel?' asked Daudet.

Herzl could not resist a mild thrust.

'No. I don't think so. I shall write something for adults. That would be better.'

'I think you are making a mistake. A novel goes a very long way. Look what "Uncle Tom's Cabin" did for the Negro question.'

Herzl talked about his plans for the book with growing enthusiasm, until at last Daudet too became enthusiastic and began to nod his head and say: 'That's fine. That's good!'

CHAPTER FIVE

The Jewish State

IN those days many stories were being told of the generosity of a Jewish multi-millionaire, Baron Maurice de Hirsch, who was spending millions of francs in a personal attempt to alleviate Jewish suffering. Baron de Hirsch was deeply moved by the plight of the Jews in Eastern Europe, where Tsarist tyranny doomed them to a life as second-class citizens, at the mercy of the mob, harried and massacred in pogroms, and subject, at best, to many humiliating restrictions.

Hirsch had the idea of founding colonies in Argentina, where such Jews could go and start a new life. He put many millions into the project.

Herzl decided that he ought to try to convert Hirsch to his views and persuade him to use his influence and wealth for settling the Jews in the land of their fathers, in Palestine. So he wrote to the millionaire and eventually obtained an interview on Sunday morning, June 2, 1895.

He prepared very carefully for the meeting. He

had a thick wad of papers on which he had made copious notes. As he passed from footman to footman through the magnificent rooms of the Baron's mansion he kept touching the papers in his pocket to keep up his confidence.

Eventually he was shown into the billiard-room. Baron de Hirsch entered almost immediately from the writing-room adjoining. He stretched out his hand in eager welcome, asked him to wait a moment and disappeared again into the next room, where Herzl heard him consulting with the officials who managed his charities.

'If the Baron wishes to give me the impression that he thinks this is just another attempt to ask him for charity, I shall soon show him he's wrong,' Herzl told himself.

'If you can't give me at least an hour, I would prefer not to begin,' he said when Hirsch returned.

'Please carry on,' the Baron answered.

Herzl had scarcely spoken five minutes when the telephone rang. The Baron unhooked the receiver and gave strict instructions that he was not to be disturbed.

'I had no intention of becoming involved in Jewish affairs,' Herzl told de Hirsch, 'but the alarming growth of antisemitism has made me change my mind. For nearly two thousand years we have been dispersed all over the world and without a State of our own. This has led to much tragedy and degradation. If we had our own political centre again we could begin to solve our problem.'

'I take it you rule out philanthropy,' said the Baron.

'Definitely. No nation has practised charity more than the Jews. Charity undermines a people's character.'

'I agree with you.'

'Can I assume that you now think your efforts in Argentina have proved either fruitless or unsatisfactory?' Herzl asked.

'Do you wish me to answer now or later?'

'Let me develop my argument,' Herzl replied. 'How many people could you hope to settle even with your vast wealth? Some fifteen or twenty thousand? Money can't move a whole people. Only an idea can do that. Your philanthropy is proving nothing and achieving nothing.'

Baron de Hirsch had been listening with increasing impatience. Now he broke in:

'Well, what's your plan?'

'We must first make the Jewish people more confident in themselves – strong and courageous.'

Hirsch stopped Herzl with an energetic gesture. 'I disagree. Jews already try to climb too high too quickly. My whole idea is to put a brake on senseless Jewish ambitions. We have far too many intellectuals already.'

Herzl explained his plan in more detail, and the Baron remarked:

'You are far too imaginative.'

But Herzl declared again that only an idea could move people, a highly imaginative idea, to which

Hirsch answered that there were plenty of lands; there was no need to concentrate on one, and emigration was the only solution.

Herzl was exasperated. 'Who was speaking of emigration?' he almost shouted. 'I was dealing with the need to make people wish to emigrate. Here it is. Here in these notes.' He waved his sheaf of papers under de Hirsch's nose. 'I shall go to the German Emperor. He'll understand me.'

Hirsch was impressed. Herzl put the notes back in his pocket.

'I shall go to the Kaiser. I shall tell him: "We are aliens. Let us go. We're not allowed to assimilate and so we can't do so!" I shall show him that the exodus can take place without causing any social or economic disturbance.'

'Where will you get the money? Rothschild will give you only a few hundred francs,' the Baron pointed out.

Herzl gave a sarcastic laugh. 'Money? I shall get money. I shall raise a national loan of ten million marks among the Jewish people themselves.'

'Rubbish! The rich Jews will give you nothing. They're hard. They harden their hearts to the sufferings of the poor.'

'You're talking like a Socialist.'

'I am one. I'm prepared to give all I possess if others feel compelled to do likewise.'

Herzl realised that the Baron refused to see how serious the matter was. He rose to go. Now Hirsch appeared to have some misgivings. 'This will not be our last talk I hope? Shall we meet when I next return from London?' he asked.

'If you wish.'

Herzl was not too bitterly disappointed. Immediately he reached home he sat down and began a long letter to the Baron, dealing with a number of points that he had not explained sufficiently at the interview. It was hardly a tactful letter. 'You are the great Jew of money,' he wrote to the Baron, 'I am the Jew of the Spirit. So it is difficult for us to understand each other.'

He tried to make the Baron see that his scheme for raising money from the Jewish people was not rubbish. He pointed out how much was needed to move the people once an idea had fired their enthusiasm. Money was needed, transportation, food, rules and regulations, contracts and agreements with the Great Powers, transit facilities through various territories, the building of cities and farms, industries, housing. There would have to be propaganda of every kind. 'I expect,' Herzl wrote, 'you will ask me mockingly under what flag we shall move. A flag is more than a piece of rag on a pole. For a flag people will go wherever you want them to, even to the Land of Promise.'

He soon realised that he was not going to win Baron de Hirsch to his view, so he decided to try the Rothschilds. The family council was shortly to meet in Paris. He would lay his plan before them. For the next few weeks he thought of nothing else. He wrote a detailed draft covering 65 pages of his plan for settling the Jews in a reconstituted commonwealth of their own. One day he had a vision of the flag of the new Jewish State.

'I see it as a white flag with seven gold stars. The white is the purity of our new life, and the stars are seven hours of work a day–a new charter for the working man.'

Herzl rejoiced as he wrote. He saw the Jews coming home, throngs boarding the ships at the seaports. He saw their excitement as they reached the Promised Land. He saw Jews of different countries settling down side by side and ceasing to worry about their Jewish characteristics, or about the good or bad opinion of others. Now they were happy for the first time and able to live free, uncomplicated lives.

The draft was finished in five days. The problem was how to get it to the Rothschilds. He turned to Dr. Moritz Güdemann, the Chief Rabbi of Vienna, who had the ear of the Austrian branch of the family. Would he read the draft to them? He wrote:

'I have found the solution to the Jewish question. I know it sounds insane and people will call me a madman. But some day they will realise the value of what I propose.'

Güdemann was very worried about Herzl, and a medical friend, Dr. Friedrich Schiff, even thought he had lost his wits. He visited him on several occasions about this time and noted that he was dishevelled in his dress, his hair was unkempt, his beard untrimmed, his eyes wild and flashing. He was completely absorbed in the fever of creation.

Herzl asked him to take care of the telegrams and urgent messages to Güdemann. He eventually let Schiff see what he had written. When he had read it the good doctor burst into tears.

'You are sending this to Dr. Güdemann? He'll think you're ill. He'll be forced to tell your family. Do you realise what you are doing to them?'

He left the room in great distress, shaking his head sadly.

Herzl, too, had his moments of bitter doubt. So this was the reception intelligent men gave his world-shattering idea. He had persuaded no one except the well-known author, Dr. Max Nordau. Yet his deep conviction drove him on. He knew he had the answer to the Jewish question. He spent less time working for the 'Neue Freie Presse' to concentrate on his plan.

One day, when Herzl's misgivings were at their peak, Schiff came in with the accounts of what he had spent on Herzl's behalf. He had made several mistakes in simple addition and subtraction.

'Well,' thought Herzl, 'here is a man passing judgment on my sanity and he cannot add up a simple column of figures.' He regarded this as a favourable omen. He began to push his scheme with new vigour. He would not wait until Güdemann brought about the interview with the Rothschilds. He would write to Count von Bismarck, who had the ear of the Emperor of Germany.

'I believe,' he said in his letter, 'that I have found

the solution to the Jewish question. Not just a solution but THE solution, the only one.'

But what if Bismarck failed to understand him? He comforted himself with the thought that even Napoleon had failed to understand the steam-engine. 'The great rulers of mankind often fail to understand new ideas,' he reflected.

He would have been spared much of the agony he experienced during these months if he had known that he was not alone in his thinking on the Jewish question. Some of the best brains in East European Jewry had been coming to the same conclusions by a similar analysis of the facts.

There was Leo Pinsker, for example. In 1882, this physician living in Odessa had published a pamphlet called 'Auto-emancipation'. In it he had stated that the problem of the Jews arose out of their homelessness. Everywhere they were strangers, never at home. They continually accepted the hospitality of the nations but had no place in which to reciprocate. Having lost their national home, they wandered through the world like disembodied spirits. People fear ghosts; what they fear they hate, and what they hate they seek to destroy.

Pinsker had suggested that the solution to the Jewish problem was for the Jews to cease to be homeless. They must acquire a land of their own somewhere and re-establish a free Jewish nation. This would restore them to normal life and win them the respect of other nations. Jews could go to this land from countries where they were so many that they constituted a problem; from Russia, for example. Then even those who remained behind would benefit from the protection which would be extended to them from the Jewish State.

Pinsker gave details of how the scheme should be organised, and one of the results of his pamphlet was that groups of Russian Jews decided to act upon it there and then. Some made ready at once to go to Palestine and settle on the land so as to lay the foundations of the future Jewish commonwealth.

Herzl knew nothing of Pinsker's work. His own plan was more detailed and thorough. But later, when he at last read 'Auto-emancipation', he said:

'If only I had known this existed I would never have bothered with my own scheme.'

Pinsker in his turn had drawn on ideas which had begun to spread through the Jewish world. But Herzl's proposal was outstanding because of the detail and clarity with which it was drawn up as a memorandum on the problem of setting up a Jewish State. He thoroughly rewrote the draft he had submitted to the Rothschilds, and the book that resulted showed exactly how the proposed Jewish State would come into being step by step. He was, moreover, determined to find means of getting to the world of practical politics and organisation, and doing so in a way that would change the whole course of Jewish history.

But the first step was to get his book published. He tried to interest his own paper in the proposal, but the proprietor of the 'Neue Freie Presse' would not allow a word to appear in his columns. He thought the whole theory crazy and fantastic, clinging firmly to the belief that the Jewish question would disappear as men became more enlightened. In the eyes of the 'Neue Freie Presse,' the ugly outbreaks of antisemitism then disturbing Austria would soon pass.

However, Herzl was far too valuable a contributor to the paper to be completely dropped from the staff. The 'Neue Freie Presse' continued to print his articles. This connection was essential for his livelihood. But he was at his wits' end to find a means of publicising his message of a reconstituted Jewish commonwealth. His personal reputation as a journalist was never greater than at that time. He was offered the editorship of a new official Government daily newspaper, a position which would have made him the trusted intimate of the Austrian Prime Minister. After long heart-searching he refused. He saw that he would not be able to utilise his new position to further his purpose of solving the Jewish question.

Meanwhile his book was going the rounds of the publishers, all of whom refused to touch it. He was consoled by the fact that a small group of friends and supporters was now gathering around him. There was Dr. Max Nordau, who had become world-famous through his book 'Degeneration'. There was a businessman, Dr. David Wolffsohn, who became his closest ally, friend and supporter. Wolffsohn was warm-hearted and generous and his support of Herzl gave him a feeling of companionship which was of inestimable value.

When the 'Neue Freie Presse' made it clear that no persuasion would move them to publish an account of Herzl's scheme, he asked for several months' leave in order to travel to Paris and London to study Jewish life and see what was being done to ease the Jewish problem. He went to Paris and saw the Chief Rabbi of France. Rabbi Zadok Kahn was only theoretically interested in the idea of restoring the Jewish State. As soon as he realised that the idea of working for such a State might indicate that French Jewry was not 100 per cent patriotic, he shied away from the issue. So did the committee of rabbis Zadok Kahn had invited to meet Herzl.

Dr. Nordau gave him an introduction to the famous Anglo-Jewish writer, Israel Zangwill, who also was interested in the Jewish problem. Zangwill was in close touch with a group of influential Jews in London who had studied the question and believed that its solution was to be found in the establishment of a Jewish commonwealth. So Herzl went off to London, where he met Zangwill. The chief result of their meeting was that he was given a number of introductions to prominent men who might be sympathetic to his general point of view.

He called on Chief Rabbi Hermann Adler, who received him hurriedly but with friendliness. Only later did he attack Herzl and call him 'an adventurer'. Meanwhile, he gave him a list of names which included Lord Rothschild and Sir Samuel Montagu,

M.P., the Rev. Simeon Singer, Mr. Asher Myers, the Editor of 'The Jewish Chronicle', and Colonel A. E. Goldsmid. As soon as Herzl expounded his views the colonel exclaimed: 'This is the idea of my life. We shall work for the restoration of Israel.' Herzl spoke to the Maccabaeans, a club of prominent Jews, who received him politely, but without any marked enthusiasm for his views, which they felt might call in question their British patriotism. But there was one practical result. Asher Myers asked him for an article, and so the gist of Herzl's book appeared in the columns of the widely-read organ of Anglo-Jewry four weeks before its publication in book form.

Herzl was encouraged by his visit to Britain. He saw that it was no use going from individual to individual. He must get his ideas over to the world. He revised the draft of his book very carefully and finally persuaded a small publisher in Vienna to produce an edition of 3,000 copies. The book was called 'Der Judenstaat' and the English translation which quickly followed was entitled 'The Jewish State – An Attempt at a Modern Solution of the Jewish Question'.

It began with a simple assertion. The Jews, Herzl wrote, are a people, one people. This in itself was a revolutionary idea to come from a Western Jew like Herzl. It meant that the Jews of Africa, of Russia, of the ghettoes – gaberdines, sidelocks, beards and all – together with the bankers of London, Paris, Berlin and New York, were one people joined in one lot and one destiny. He went on to say that despite all the great contributions made by Jews to the lands in which they lived, they were neither left in peace or accepted. There was always the possibility of persecution and exclusion. He declared that the Jewish people could never be destroyed. Some parts of the nation fell away, as branches wither on a tree; the root remained and lived on.

It was no use looking for local solutions to the Jewish question. If the Jews tried to improve themselves that would not help them to overcome the evil prejudices of their enemies, who would still try to destroy them when it suited them. The nations of the world would not let the Jews be fully absorbed into them. In any case, that assumed Jews wished to be absorbed, and they did not.

In his introduction Herzl asserted that the causes of Jewish suffering throughout the world were identical and therefore a common solution had to be sought for them everywhere. The universal answer was to set up a Jewish State again; to restore the Jewish people to a land of their own, where they could live a free, independent life according to their own laws.

The problem, however, was not simply a Jewish problem. It was one which affected the whole world. Therefore one could look forward confidently to the world's assistance in solving the problem.

He then proceeded to outline the practical steps needed to restore Jewish statehood.

A Jewish company would have to be set up to

organise the sale of the property of Jews preparing to emigrate to the State and to take care of settlement within its borders.

An International Society of Jews must be organised to represent Jewry throughout the world and, in accordance with international law, to acquire a territory for the resettlement of the Jewish people.

'Judenstaat' then laid down definite rules for the emigration. The poorest would go first, then the middle-class would follow. Details were given of how settlement and labour were to be handled in the new commonwealth. There would be a central body to distribute the land. There would be an overall development plan. A council of jurists would formulate the laws. Details were given of the social legislation that would be introduced. For example there would be a seven-hour working day.

'The Jews who want it,' said Herzl, 'will have their State.'

CHAPTER SIX

First Steps in Diplomacy

HERZL'S 'Judenstaat' had repercussions all over the world. The work had such effect, not because of anything new in it, but because of the man who said it, the daring manner in which he put his case, and his absolute conviction that what he said was feasible and would come about.

Men had been trying variants of his solution for over a generation. In Eastern Europe there was an organisation called Hovevei Zion, Lovers of Zion, with branches throughout the Tsarist Empire and with affiliated organisations in other countries. This movement had been sending a trickle of Jews to Palestine, where some land was bought from the Turks on which they sought to establish themselves in their ancestral homeland. By the time 'Judenstaat' appeared some eighteen colonies had been set up. These consisted mainly of struggling farmers who employed Arab labour. They had for the most part been subsidised by the munificence of Baron Edmond de Rothschild and could not continue to exist without this aid. These colonists were dissatisfied and depressed and did not seem to be making much progress.

Some members of the Hovevei Zion severely criticised the way in which the colonies had been established. Asher Ginsberg, who wrote under the pen-name of Ahad Ha'am (One of the People) suggested that colonisation was not so important as the need to free Jews from the desire to assimilate by reviving their national spirit and idealism. In any case, the Turkish Government, which controlled Palestine, imposed restrictions on the Jews who had settled there. It restricted their immigration, and since the colonies could develop only if a benevolent Turkish Government would allow them to do so, it was obvious that they could quite easily be strangled without notice should an ill-disposed régime decide to end them.

So the Hovevei Zion, which had a vested interest in these colonies, was not too certain about the consequences of Herzl's sudden appearance on the scene. Some of its members thought his openly declared intention to ask Governments to assist in the creation of a Jewish State might inspire Turkey to liquidate their work in Palestine. But there were others, who now called themselves Zionists, who saw in Herzl's bold statements just the new courage and new inspiration that were essential if the movement was to begin to attain practical goals. Many of these rallied to his support.

The rich and powerful Jews of the world, led by

most of their influential rabbis, violently opposed Herzl. They looked upon the idea of a Jewish State as sheer lunacy. Pamphlets were written proving it to be an absurdity. One man, Dr. Ernst, suggested that for Jews to flee from Europe was an act of cowardly desertion in the face of their enemies. The German and Austrian press ridiculed Herzl and gave him all sorts of nicknames. Many orthodox Jews called him a blasphemer, asserting that if God wanted the Jews to return to Palestine and be a people again He would bring it about in His own good time, by His own means, and without human intervention. Some Jews attacked Herzl because the credulous began to accept him as a sort of false Messiah. However, all the Jewish student clubs of Vienna rallied to him and asked him to head the movement for the establishment of the Jewish State.

The publicity, good and bad, around 'Judenstaat' made its mark on the Jewish world. The masses everywhere began to regard Herzl as almost Messianic. With his tall, commanding presence, his piercing eyes, his full, black beard he looked like a legendary figure stepping out of past history. He walked with the nobility and dignity of a prince among men. Here was one of the great intellectuals of German culture, who had the world of Western journalism at his feet, deliberately choosing to forfeit the glittering prizes within his reach in order to become a servant dedicated to lead the Jewish people from exile into statehood.

Leading Jews of Palestine issued a memorandum

endorsing his plan. Among the signatories who agreed to follow his leadership were men of the calibre of Eliezer Ben Yehuda, the scholar who had turned the moribund Hebrew language into a living tongue. 'Be strong,' they wrote to him, 'and of good courage. Be firm in the struggle for our just rights, for our dignity, for the freedom and happiness of our people.'

In the East End of London and the East Side of New York, the poor Jewish masses, who had only recently emigrated to escape the monstrous tyranny of the Tsars and who were now struggling in the sweat-shops of these great metropolises to establish a new foothold, were transformed by Herzl's call for a new Jewish pride. Now they lived in the hope of a future in which their great past would be revived. They formed societies and groups to support Herzl.

Now he found that he must forgo the rôle of thinker and become a man of action. He could not rest content with having brought his solution to the notice of the world. It was not enough for him to refute brilliantly the bitter criticisms of his opponents, particularly the assimilationist rabbis and quite a number of the Orthodox whom he dubbed 'Protest Rabbiner', to distinguish them from men like Rabbi Dr. Ruelf, who supported him. Now he had to organise a machine to put his ideas into practice. He had to undertake the rôles of speaker, organiser, diplomat and statesman. He had foreseen all this; his plan was ready. If the Jewish people were, as he claimed, one people throughout the world, they must have one world-wide organisation to give practical expression to their aims. And he must find a means of gaining the support of the world generally for his plan. He believed that mankind would wish for a solution of the Jewish question because it was necessary for the peace and stability of society.

'If I go ahead,' he told himself, 'those who are hesitant and doubtful will come along with me as soon as they see that the movement is really under way.'

On March 10, 1896, he was sitting in his room when the door opened suddenly and a wild-looking, strangely attired British clergyman burst in. He had the appearance of a Biblical prophet; a bearded face, plentiful, shaggy hair and an air of other-worldly excitement.

'I am full of enthusiasm for your project,' he began at once. 'It is the fulfilment of Biblical prophecy. Look. I have written on the subject myself.'

He produced a volume and thrust it into Herzl's hands. It was called 'The Restoration of the Jews to Palestine according to the Prophets'.

In this volume, the Reverend William Hechler, for that was the visitor's name, proved by texts from the Scriptures that the restoration of the Jews was to take place in 1897. He had seen Herzl's book and took it as the first definite sign that the prophecy was ripe for fulfilment. He wanted to help. As Chaplain to the British Embassy in Vienna he could bring

'Judenstaat' to the attention of important princes and potentates. Herzl realised that Hechler's visit might well prove providential. The clergyman had been tutor to the family of the Grand Duke of Baden and was confident that he could arrange for an interview between him and the German Emperor.

Others, too, came forward. There was a Polish nobleman, Count Philip Michael, Ritter von Nevlinski, a former diplomat, now a journalist. He became Herzl's friend and coached him in diplomatic procedure. It was he who eventually introduced him to the King of Bulgaria and several Turkish statesmen, thus setting him on the path which eventually led to his meeting with the Sultan.

Hechler soon introduced Herzl to the ruler of Baden. Herzl told the Grand Duke quite frankly that it was very important for the success of the Society of Jews "that he should have Royal support."

'Your Highness,' he said, 'it will add to the success and prestige of our movement and thus make emigration so much easier to organise.'

His next interview was with the Papal Nuncio in Vienna. That dignitary was not impressed, but the interview gave Herzl more confidence. The great ones of the earth or their close representatives were beginning to submit his plan to serious discussion. He was no longer considered a madman. He heard that Gladstone, the veteran British statesman, had read with interest a copy of 'The Jewish State' which Sir Samuel Montagu had given him.

On June 9, 1896, Nevlinski reported that he had

just been to London, where he sensed a strong feeling in diplomatic circles that Turkey was disintegrating as a State.

'There is only one hope for the Sultan to preserve his Empire,' Nevlinski said. 'He must come to terms with the Young Turks and agree upon reforms.'

'It seems to me,' Herzl answered, 'that with Jewish aid he might be offered the financial means to bring about such reforms. Let the Sultan give us that part of his dominion known as Palestine, and in return we shall take care of his finances, put his economy in order and win him the good opinion of the whole world.'

After further discussion Nevlinski was instructed to write to Constantinople and try to obtain for Herzl an interview with the Sultan. This was not achieved, but Herzl made the journey to the Turkish capital, where he met some of the ruler's principal ministers. The scheme he broached to them was a bold one. In return for a broad concession to settle Jews in Palestine and restore a Jewish State there, he would undertake to save the Turkish Empire from bankruptcy.

The negotiations at the Turkish Court were long and involved. Out of his own pocket Herzl bribed and feasted the Court dignitaries, but he could not get near the Sultan. At length he received an indirect reply through one of the ruler's councillors:

'The Sultan states that Herzl would be well advised to drop the whole matter.'

The exact words used were: 'The dominion of

Turkey is not my personal possession but that of the Turkish people. I cannot give any portion of it away. It would be better for the Jews to save their milliards!'

Herzl was forced to drop the attempt for the time being. He started back to Vienna. On the way he stopped at Sofia, the capital of Bulgaria. There he was met by a committee of Zionists, and enthusiastic crowds of Jews greeted them as they passed through the streets. He attended the synagogue, which was crowded. He stood reverently before the Holy Ark. The congregation clamoured for him to speak. He was at a loss; to turn to them would mean turning his back on the sanctuary.

One man called out, 'Don't worry. Your work is sacred. Turn round to us.' As he walked down the aisle men clutched at his coat and tried to kiss his hand.

Next he visited England in the hope of winning the support of the strong local Hovevei Zion group. He also wanted to win over the great leaders of Anglo-Jewry, who had privately expressed their sympathy. He offered to resign his leadership of the movement to Lord Rothschild if he would come out in favour of mass immigration into Palestine. But he had made enemies of the Rothschild family and they openly opposed him. The wealthy members of Anglo-Jewry followed their lead.

On the other hand, the masses, as everywhere, attended his meetings in the East End with greater enthusiasm than ever. He began to realise that he would never attain his goal if he depended on the wealthy Jews. Their stake in Jewry within the nations was too great and they had hypnotised themselves into believing that the unsatisfactory features of the Jewish situation would clear with time. In Paris, Baron Edmond de Rothschild feared the effect of a sudden influx of hordes of poor Jews on his carefully nurtured colonies. He flatly rejected the idea of obtaining a concession for Palestine from the Sultan for a sum of money.

Herzl decided that if he failed to obtain financial support from a few wealthy Jews, a very large number of small contributions from less wealthy and even poor Jews would yield the same result. On July 21, 1896, he wrote:

'There is only one answer to our problem. We must organise the masses.'

Next day he spoke at a meeting of Russian Jewish students in London. He called on them to form themselves into groups in support of his movement. On the morrow he left for Vienna, where he immediately set about the task of organising a general conference of all who were interested in his movement. He wrote to David Wolffsohn and asked him to bring in the German Zionists.

'We shall begin at once to convene a Zionist Congress,' he said. 'That will be our answer to Rothschild and the other millionaires.'

While he was busily engaged in these tasks he found time to consult his physician. The strain of the constant journeys, interviews, speeches and public appearances was taking too great a toll of his strength. The doctor diagnosed heart disease. Herzl accepted the verdict in silence and continued his efforts with even greater energy. If his life was to be cut short, that was all the more reason why he should work harder than ever.

As the date of the Zionist Congress drew near the tumult of opposition mounted almost to hysteria. The 'Neue Freie Presse', which had promised Herzl it would publish reports on Zionism, maintained a silence. He was forced to start his own newspaper, which he called 'Die Welt' (The World). He spent 25,000 florins of his personal fortune in launching this organ of the World Zionist Organisation. It continued to exist, first in German, and later in Hebrew, until after the Jewish State came into being in 1948.

One of Herzl's reasons for convening a Zionist Congress was to convince the hesitant wealthy Jews that a unified world Jewry was a reality. Perhaps then they might be persuaded to finance the mass emigration of Jews to Palestine. He gave his personal attention to the organisation of groups in Vienna; in Germany, England, Galicia, Bulgaria and other places friends were busy forming societies. The most important leaders of Palestine Jewry joined, and support came from distant Canada, America and South Africa.

But the opposition was equally vigorous. The Hovevei Zion in London, which believed that settlement in Palestine should be done gradually and that theatrical activities, like a Zionist Congress, might provoke restrictive Turkish measures, refused their support. Herzl brushed their objections aside.

'The Zionist Congress must and will take place,' he announced.

His vigorous drive to bring about this conference alarmed the assimilationists. They recalled that when Napoleon emancipated French Jewry, as one of the conditions of their new equality he had forbidden Jewish nationality. They did not grasp the essential fact that emancipation on conditions is not real emancipation. They all called Herzl mad for proposing to call Jews together from all parts of the world to an international meeting. It would be said that Jews were not good Frenchmen, Englishmen or Germans. They would be proclaiming themselves members of a peculiar and distinct nation and demanding that Governments of the world should recognise them as such. This, the assimilationists said, spelled suicide for the Jews. All their rights and privileges would be jeopardised. They had no option but to fight Herzl by every means at their command.

Foremost among this opposition were leading rabbis, who claimed that Zionism distorted the ideals of Judaism. Herzl counter-attacked vigorously. No one has asked you to join, he said. Those who did not feel they were one with the Jewish people on the march could stay where they were. No one was forcing them to do anything.

He pushed on with his plans. Originally the Congress was to have been held in Munich; but when the Jewish community there officially objected, the meeting place was changed to Basle, in Switzerland. And there, on August 29, 1897, the first Zionist Congress finally assembled. Herzl had taken the first decisive step, after publication of 'Judenstaat', to unite the Jewish people in its effort to reclaim its lost homeland and statehood.

CHAPTER SEVEN

The First Zionist Congress

IT was a tiring Theodor Herzl who, with a few friends, set out for Basle in that last week of August, 1897. Yet never before had he felt so capable of tremendous, almost superhuman effort. The journalist and writer had become a man of action. Not simply action in the diplomatic field, but action in his capacity as the chief administrator of a great organisation.

The hall had to be booked and provision made for the offices, committee rooms and secretaries. The press had to be accommodated so that journalists could send the Congress message to the ends of the earth. Men, and some women, were coming from many lands. They had to be looked after and made to feel the importance of the work they were doing not only for themselves but for the whole of Jewry.

There was the weekly newspaper 'Die Welt' to supervise. For a long time now this paper had been Herzl's own responsibility. All unsigned items and articles came from his pen.

Each delegation had its own peculiar anxieties. Thus, the Russians, the most passionately devoted of all Zionists, were afraid lest something might be said which would bring down the wrath of the Tsar's secret police upon them. The Palestinian delegates had a more complex problem. They wanted to see a new path blazed in Zionism, but they did not wish to alienate Baron Rothschild lest he should cease his philanthropy. The colonies were still largely dependent upon his munificence. They were also afraid that something indiscreet said at the Congress might provoke the Sultan of Turkey into some act of tyranny which could put an end to the small beginnings made in Palestine. Herzl had also to contend with his anti-Zionist Jewish opponents, who spared no calumny or vilification in order to discount in advance whatever decisions the Congress might take.

There were lighter moments to relieve the strain. A few hours before the first session was to commence, someone at the committee asked:

'What flag shall the Congress have?'

'Let the blue-and-white *tallit* [prayer-shawl] be our flag,' David Wolffsohn suggested.

They added the Star of David to broad bands of blue and white, and that became the Congress banner. As the delegates entered the hall they saw over the platform a great flag and beside it the words, in German, 'First Zionist Congress'. This flag has remained the standard of the Jewish people to this day.

Herzl insisted that all delegates must attend the opening session in formal dress. As they stood up one could see that this was a gathering of men and women from many lands. There were the wealthy from the Western countries, comfortable and at ease in their tail-coats. There were people from England, from France, the Austro-Hungarian Empire, the Russian Empire, the Scandinavian countries, from Africa and Algeria, from Egypt and Palestine.

The committee sat on the platform at a long table covered with green baize cloth. The press table was crowded with reporters from many of the world's most important newspapers. The public galleries were filled with Jewish spectators and distinguished Gentile well-wishers whom Herzl had invited.

The Chairman, an old Zionist from Rumania, opened the proceedings with three knocks of his gavel, and then pronounced the ancient Hebrew benediction, *Sheheheyanu,* simple words hallowed by Jewish religious tradition and said when something new gives cause for thankfulness to God.

'Blessed art Thou, O Lord our God,' Dr. Lippe intoned, 'who hast kept us alive and privileged us to reach this moment.'

And the delegates cried: 'Amen.'

Herzl rose to address the delegates. He stood waiting for the storm of applause to subside. It was several minutes before he could be heard.

'We have an important task before us. We have met here to lay the foundation-stone of the house that will some day shelter the Jewish people. The matter is so tremendous that only the simplest words will suffice to describe it. . . .'

He then went on to indicate that modern methods of communication and the modern organisation of life made it possible to reconstitute the Jewish nation. The first step was a strong, unified, world-wide organisation. . . . The Zionists had to bring the Jewish question openly before the world. . . . 'We have to aim at securing legal, international guarantees for our work. . . .'

'At this Congress we bring to the Jewish people an organisation it did not possess before. . . . It is a vital necessity. Our movement is too great to be a tool of any individual's lust for power or desire for glory. If we wish it to succeed it has to rise above the personal level. Our Congress will eternally endure, not just until the hour of redemption but beyond it. Now we meet in a free and friendly city. . . . Where shall we be next year?

'Our Congress has to be the glory and pride of the whole House of Israel.'

As he spoke, he was aware that he was making history. . . . For the first time the will of the Jewish people throughout the world, in so far as it could be democratically declared, was being expressed. Here was assembled the greatest and most representative body of Jews that had ever been brought together since the destruction of the last Jewish commonwealth 1827 years before. It plainly asserted a principle long forgotten and abandoned by modern Jewry. Many years before, Napoleon had assembled the notables of French Jewry to tell them of their emancipation, and had said that as a people they were entitled to nothing; they were granted their privileges solely on the grounds of religion. Their leaders had agreed to this condition. Now Herzl brought an even more representative group of Jews together for the express purpose of affirming the very principle of nationality their forebears had only recently renounced. They were making the revolutionary declaration that they were entitled to everything that the world has to give to all other peoples. And the first thing they wanted was a Jewish State.

The Congress rapidly got down to the business of organising Jewry for its coming statehood. Some of the things done at Basle that year brought sneers of contempt to the lips of the Jewish noblemen and millionaires, but Herzl's vision was clearer than theirs.

The Congress adopted a resolution, which has become known in Jewish history as 'The Basle Programme'. It covered the following points:

The task of Zionism is to secure for the Jewish people in Palestine a publicly recognised, legally secured homeland.

To achieve this Congress decides to:

1. Encourage the systematic settlement of Palestine with Jewish agricultural workers, labourers and artisans.
2. Organise and unite the Jewish people by the creation of groups in various countries whose object would be to foster the aims of the

movement. These groups were to be organised in accordance with the laws of their respective countries.

3. Dedicate itself to strengthening Jewish consciousness and national feeling.
4. Organise political efforts so as to obtain the support of the various Governments of the world for the aims of Zionism.

It is interesting to look back on this programme and to reflect that if one were to summarise the actual steps that led to the emergence of the State of Israel in 1948, one need only repeat the four points laid down by Herzl and his Congress in 1897.

All Jewish people throughout the world who supported the aims of Zionism were asked to join the organisation, signing a declaration that they agreed with the Basle Programme and paying a Shekel, about one shilling, to the World Zionist Organisation. In the first year over 100,000 Jews made this symbolic payment for membership. The Shekel, in ancient times, was the poll-tax every Jew all over the world, like their brethren still living in the then State of Israel, paid to the Temple treasury to finance the regular service of worship in the sanctuary. In Herzl's time and since, it has meant that no matter where Jews are scattered they have had a voice, through democratic vote based on the Shekel, in deciding just what form the building of the Jewish State should take.

It was at this Congress that Professor Hermann Schapira first suggested a Jewish National Fund.

Jews all over the world were to give regular sums, no matter how small, to be used for buying land in Palestine. Such land would be the eternal and inalienable property of the Jewish people. This proposal was not actually carried until the Fifth Zionist Congress. But it was the origin of the Jewish National Fund which, in the course of the years, was to buy most of the land on which the State of Israel was subsequently founded.

Another proposal was to establish a Jewish National Bank to finance the movement. This was agreed. It took a few years to organise the Bank, and many of its shares were bought by poor Jews living then in direst poverty in small villages of Eastern Europe. Today this bank is the largest in the State of Israel. In the course of time its name was changed to the Anglo-Palestine Bank, and after Israel came into being to Bank Leumi, the National Bank. It is still the banker to the World Zionist Organisation. It issued the first currency of the new Israel.

Another dream mentioned at the Congress was the establishment of a Hebrew University. This, too, was realised in Jerusalem a generation later. One of the most dramatic developments during the proceedings was the change of heart of many important rabbis, headed by the Chief Rabbi of Basle. They told Herzl they were satisfied that Judaism would be strengthened by Zionism and pledged their support.

Concerning the Congress Herzl made only a brief entry in his diary:

'It is not necessary for me to write down what

happened yesterday. Others are already doing that. I was quite tranquil. Many were moved to the depths of their souls. I was calm, as one should be when things which have been carefully planned become realities.'

In order to concentrate on his Zionist work, he had consistently neglected his family. His children were always longing for the infrequent visits of their father, now a rare and almost legendary figure, but who loved them dearly and was loved by them. The day after Congress opened he suddenly felt it was all worth while just because of them. He was sitting in the seat of honour reserved for the President of the World Zionist Organisation, to which office he had been elected by acclamation. Before him was his mail. It included the very first letter ever written to him by his son Hans, now six years old. Tears started to his eyes. For the first time he was shaken out of his calm. There, at the President's table, he took up his pen and wrote Congress postcards to his parents, his wife and children. He felt a little self-conscious.

'This is a sacred and historic place,' he told himself. 'It will go down in history for what shall come from here.' He smiled somewhat wryly. 'This is the first act of childish self-indulgence I have allowed myself amid all the tumult of the past two years.'

When he returned to Vienna a week later he was so tired that he could hardly hold his pen. Now and again he sustained himself by the achievements of Congress. That day, he wrote:

'If I have to sum up the first Zionist Congress in one sentence, it is this: In Basle I founded the Jewish State. If I were to say this in public I would be greeted by hoots of loud laughter from all sides. But perhaps within five years, perhaps within fifty, everyone will recognise this fact. A State is founded on the people's will for statehood, even on the will of one person if he is strong. . . . The territory is simply the physical embodiment of that will. . . . Because it is an abstract will, many do not see it that way. . . . I have set the minds of the Jewish people in the direction of statehood. I have aroused their national will. I have given them their National Assembly.'

His prophecy was correct almost to the day. Fifty years later, on November 29, 1947, a different kind of international meeting came together. It was the General Assembly of the United Nations at Lake Success, New York, in plenary session to discuss the problem of the Jewish section of Palestine, which had grown from the eighteen small villages of Herzl's day to a population of 650,000. In the evening of November 29, the delegates voted on a resolution declaring that a Jewish State was to be established in Palestine, and recognised by the nations of the world sitting in their highest tribunal. The resolution was carried. The Jewish State came into being on May 15, 1948, six months later. It was strong enough to fight off simultaneous attacks from all the surrounding Arab nations and Egypt. Herzl had proved to be a true prophet. He had revived the people's will and that will had led it to overcome all opposition and to renew its nationality in the homeland which it now proudly named 'The State of Israel'. 'If only you will it, it will not be a fable,' Herzl had said, and history endorsed his statement.

CHAPTER EIGHT

The Grand Duke Helps

YET he had to accept the fact that while Congress had made a revolutionary impression on the Jewish world, it had not won over all that world. He was now the unquestioned leader of the Jewish masses, but his bitter opponents among the Western assimilationist Jews remained unconvinced, and many of the intellectual leaders of Zionism in Eastern Europe still opposed him, yet gradually his idealism, conviction and the speedy growth of the Zionist movement captured their followers. He knew how important it was to secure the allegiance of the British and French sections of the Hovevei Zion movement. In the event this was the path of wisdom. The Zionists of the West European, and later the Western world, though numerically less than those of Eastern Europe, played an increasingly important part in support of Herzl. After his time, they gradually laid the foundations, especially in the political and financial sphere, for most of the developments leading to the emergence of Israel that followed so swiftly. At this period, however, Herzl's immediate problem was how to win the support of the Russian Zionists. These men had come as a revelation to him when he met them at Congress. He saw that they were the focal point of Jewry. They represented millions of people, inseparably attached to their Jewish past, and with an unmistakable belief in their future. They knew Hebrew, the Bible and the ancient sources of Jewish law, which they had studied as children. They felt instinctively that the only direction in which Jewish life should move was towards the return to the homeland. Now he had met the leaders of Russian Jewry. Herzl was filled with admiration for them. They included great scholars, professors, engineers, teachers, doctors and mathematicians; they spoke several languages; they were thoroughly at home in European culture and were equally well versed in Jewish traditional lore. Their loyalties were wholly to the Jewish people, and their one desire was to bring relief to their peoples and give them hope of a better future.

Many of them, it is true, disagreed with Herzl. Some felt that the work of colonisation ought to go forward quietly and unobtrusively; others later thought he was neglecting this field in favour of diplomacy. One of the greatest leaders of Russian Jewry was Ahad Haam, a great philosopher and essayist. He believed the trouble with the Jewish people was that it had lost its understanding of, and loyalty to, Judaism, and its spiritual heritage. It had given these up for the good things the nations offered it under emancipation. Now Jews were unhappy, not because of antisemitism, but because they were enslaved to their ignorance and desire to live the life of other nations rather than their own. Ahad Haam called this process 'Slavery in the midst of Freedom'. He thought that by talking of reconstructing Jewish nationhood through political action Herzl was driving Jewry further along the road of error. He believed the Jews must first find their soul, and only then would they find their way back to nationhood. In any case the establishment of a Jewish political centre was in his view a purely secondary consideration. Its purpose must be to act as the spiritual centre of Jewry stimulating a spiritual revival among the scattered members of Jewry all over the world.

Ahad Haam was not quite fair to Herzl, who had made it perfectly clear that he believed a return to Zion must be preceded by a return to Judaism. It was Herzl who, from the very beginning, had stressed that only ideas could move a people to become a nation.

The masses of Jewry understood Herzl, for he understood them. The unity of the Jewish people which he talked about and which he sought to restore as a practical instrument, was for them a very real thing. They would instinctively recognise another Jew as a brother, no matter where he lived or what language he spoke. In contrast with the assimilated Jews, who were trying to prove that they were really Frenchmen, Englishmen or Germans of

Jewish faith, the mass of Jews looked upon other Jews everywhere as their own brethren. So they understood and worshipped Herzl.

This did not mean that all the Zionists, while supporting him generally, accepted his views entirely. Many did not. Soon clearly defined groups or parties began to form who wanted the Promised Land to be given a special character. The deeply religious Zionists felt that the emphasis must be placed on making the Jewish State a centre of Orthodox Judaism, to ensure that the customs and rituals of Judaism would be rigidly observed. There were Socialists and Social Democrats who wanted to build from the very beginning on Socialist principles. There were others who refused to lay down any political doctrine, but had their own theories about colonisation. It was not until 1903, at the Sixth Zionist Congress, that some of these trends crystallised into definite political parties, and the Mizrachi (religious Zionists) and Poale Zion (Socialist Zionists) emerged.

But Herzl's main demands were accepted. They had to have the Bank in order to provide funds for the movement. Membership must be expanded so that all the forces in the world working for the restoration of Zion could pool their resources in one organisation strong enough to achieve it. Herzl set about cementing all these elements into a unity, trying to bring in those who were still outside while at the same time fighting his enemies by ceaseless propaganda. He concentrated on two internal aims;

the establishment of the Bank, and preparations for the Second Congress. In the larger spheres he pressed on with his attempts to get an audience of the Sultan and treat with him for a charter or some other form of legal sanction for Jews to settle in large numbers in Palestine and establish the Jewish State. He believed his best approach to the Sultan was through the German Emperor, to whom Turkey was greatly indebted. He felt he could persuade him that a Jewish State, under German protection in the Middle East, would be of service to Germany's imperial interests in that area.

But his first concern was for the Bank, for unless he had the money to back his schemes it was no use talking. He tried one great Jewish banker after another and met with cold refusal. So he decided that the masses of Jewry would have to subscribe for the shares which would provide the Bank's capital. He was ably assisted by the energetic David Wolffsohn, and three days before the second Congress was due to assemble, on August 25, 1898, he was able to call a preliminary meeting to report on the progress of the Bank's affairs.

The Second Congress opened on August 28. In retrospect it was notable for the presence of a number of people who later became prominent in the Zionist movement. There was a young Russian delegate, Chaim Weizmann, who followed Herzl as President of the World Zionist Organisation and became the first President of the State of Israel. There was a journalist, Nahum Sokolow, who had attended the First Congress as the representative of a newspaper but had not been a delegate. He, too, later became President of the World Zionist Organisation. It was these who, on November 2, 1917, obtained from the British Government through Mr. Balfour a declaration recognising the right of the Jews to build a national home in Palestine. It is significant that, already at the First and Second Congresses, men who were to play a decisive rôle in realising Herzl's dreams had enlisted under his banner.

The First Congress had assembled 197 delegates; at the Second they totalled 400 representing 913 groups. The Congress was told that the plans for the Bank had been drawn up. It received the first official World Zionist Organisation report on colonisation in Palestine. This was presented by Leo Motzkin, whom Herzl had sent to make an investigation. From the discussion which followed important principles with regard to colonisation emerged. It was decided that an attempt should be made to move some unproductive Jews living on charity from Jerusalem into colonies and settlements where they could live by the labour of their own hands.

Herzl was completely exhausted when the Congress closed on September 2. The sessions had been stormy. There had been bitter debates with some of the rabbis who demanded guarantees on religious issues. There was a sharp division of opinion over the Bank and methods of colonisation. All these had to be smoothed out by Herzl and the agreement secured was largely due to his personal efforts. The labour took a heavy toll of his health. He was weary almost to death; but his energy and spirit were not impaired. Accompanied by the faithful Hechler he went straight from the Congress to the island of Mainau to have an audience of the Grand Duke of Baden. He hoped that this would lead directly to a meeting with the German Emperor.

It was 10 a.m. on September 4 when they arrived at the ducal palace. The Duke was not ready to receive them and they were asked to wait in a small room on the ground floor. They sat watching the brilliant procession of soldiers, gorgeously dressed footmen and courtiers passing in and out. Suddenly one of them, in general's uniform, turned to Hechler and said: 'Hello, old fellow. What the devil are you doing here? I thought you'd decided that the end of the world was overdue.'

He was the tutor who had succeeded Hechler in the Grand Duke's family.

Punctually at noon they were shown into a room on the first floor where the Grand Duke received them very warmly. It was a friendly and informal occasion. The Duke sat with his back to the window, so his face was in deep shadow during the whole interview. Herzl, who sat facing him, had the full glare of the hot sun on him.

'I have been in touch with our diplomats,' said the Duke. 'Our German Government has sounded the Sultan on his attitude towards Zionism and he views it with favour.'

'I am delighted to hear it,' exclaimed Herzl. 'We

dispatched a telegram to the Sultan from our Congress conveying our highest esteem.'

'I have been talking about your plans at great length with His Imperial Majesty,' continued the Grand Duke. 'He has asked Count zu Eulenburg, our Ambassador in Vienna, to look into the question of the Zionist movement and to prepare a memorandum on it.'

'You wish to establish a State,' the Grand Duke mused. 'Yes. Perhaps that would be the best thing. Of course, at first it would have to be Turkish; but no one knows what time may bring about.'

Herzl turned the conversation into a discussion of how Zionism had diverted many Jews from revolutionary parties.

'In Russia, Jews are leaving the Socialist and Anarchist parties to become Zionists,' he said. 'My movement gives them an ideal in life.'

'I really must let the Russians know about this,' the Grand Duke chuckled. 'But please, tell me this. Would not certain rich Jews regard our Kaiser's support of Zionism as antisemitic, as expressing a desire that they should leave his dominions? You will recall that when there were anti-Jewish riots in Algiers the Rothschilds actually threatened the French Government that they would withdraw from France unless action was taken.'

'Your Highness,' Herzl replied, 'as soon as the influential Jews see that the German Emperor upholds Zionism, their fears of being thought anti-patriotic will disappear. In any case, we do not contemplate that all the Jews will leave for the Jewish State. Those who want to will go; the rest will remain and will become more deeply rooted in the land of their birth.'

'Very likely, very likely,' murmured the Duke.

'What is more,' Herzl continued, 'Zionism will mean the spread of German culture and influence in the East. Do you know that the proceedings of our Zionist Congresses are in the German language?'

After their interview, Herzl persisted in his efforts to obtain the interview with the Kaiser. He was received by the German Ambassador in Vienna, and emphasised that he wished the Kaiser to persuade the Sultan to open negotiations with himself. He also saw the German Foreign Minister, Von Bülow, who promised that he would consider the matter carefully.

In the meantime he visited Paris, Holland and London in an effort to speed up the formation of the Bank. After all, if the Kaiser did agree to take the Zionist movement under his wing, the next step would be direct negotiations with the Sultan concerning a concession for Palestine. For that they must have money, and money could come only through the Bank.

The strain on Herzl's heart increased with the growing pressure of affairs. Now he was fighting his illness all the time. Will-power alone kept him going. The only moments he had for relaxation were when he was travelling, although he often wrote up his diaries in the train or on board ship.

Once, as he was journeying through the beautiful, cultivated landscape of Holland, his thoughts went back thirteen years, when, as a young man, he had made the same journey.

'At that time,' he reflected, 'I saw things only from the outside, superficially. Now the whole world talks to me in a different language.'

As he looked out of the carriage window suddenly a great city appeared out of the flat plain that extended without even a hillock. They were approaching The Hague.

'This is a sign,' he thought, 'that the human will alone can raise up a metropolis. All one has to do is point one's finger at a certain spot and say, "Arise and become a living city!" And behold, a new town stands before your eyes!'

At that moment, the whole of Holland seemed to illustrate what men could achieve on the most difficult and, at first sight, unrewarding territory. He smiled to himself. 'It is strange how everything I see these days stimulates me to think of the idea which has taken possession of all my being.'

CHAPTER NINE

Herzl and the Kaiser

IN Amsterdam Herzl received a message to call at the German Consulate. There he was given another message, from Count zu Eulenburg, saying that the German Emperor (known as the Kaiser) was prepared to take the Zionist movement under his protection and that, during his forthcoming visit to Palestine, he would be willing to receive a deputation led by Herzl in Jerusalem.

Herzl was delighted. He quickly called Wolffsohn and others of the executive into consultation. But for him this moment of triumph was attended with difficulties. In order to go to Palestine he would have to get the agreement of his employers of the 'Neue Freie Presse', who were more bitterly opposed than ever to his Zionist activities and might dismiss him if he became too involved in international politics. He had no source of income apart from his writing. He had spent every penny he possessed on 'Die Welt'. On the other hand, the summons to meet the Kaiser could not be ignored.

He went for a solitary cycle ride to Scheveningen. The exercise and the beauty of the evening along the promenade soothed him. In Amsterdam he saw Jewish children playing in the street and singing the Dutch national anthem.

'In ten years' time these same youngsters will be singing the hymn of Zion,' he told himself.

One result of the communication from zu Eulenburg was that at a mass meeting in London that week Herzl forsook his usual caution. He spoke to the 10,000 Jews who had gathered inside and outside the hall in the East End as though a Messianic deliverance were at hand. 'I declare today,' he told them, 'that I fervently believe the time is very close when the Jewish people will be definitely on the march. . . . We are the guardians of the truth. Follow that truth and do not forsake it until our people arrive at better times.'

On his return to Vienna a series of difficult and delicate negotiations took place with Count zu Eulenburg, the Foreign Minister von Bülow, and the Chancellor Hohenlohe. He got the impression that while the Kaiser was genuinely in favour of the aims of Zionism, those two statesmen, who advised him on policy, were working against the movement. They told Herzl he would be received not in Jerusalem but in Constantinople.

'But what about Jerusalem?' he asked.

'There will be only one reception,' von Bülow answered as he rose to leave the conference.

On October 13 the Zionist deputation took the

Orient Express to Constantinople. There they found that the atmosphere was not as friendly as they had anticipated. They could not even be sure whether the Kaiser would receive them.

Time was running very short. Unless Herzl could see the Kaiser by October 18, he would have to go on to Palestine without arranging anything definite. The last boat he could catch to arrive there in time was leaving the next morning.

It was not until the afternoon of that last day that he received a sudden summons to present himself at the palace which had been put at the Kaiser's disposal. It had been an anxious day. Quite early Herzl had taken out his formal morning coat and had it brushed and put ready. The previous day he had sent a last plea to Count zu Eulenburg to arrange the audience with the Kaiser before he left for Palestine. Then he could sit and wait.

At 3.15 p.m. the hotel porter entered Herzl's room. Trembling with excitement, he announced: 'A messenger has come with a communication to Dr. Herzl from His Imperial Majesty.'

Herzl hurriedly put on his coat and hastened downstairs. However, the messenger only left a formal note notifying him that his audience was to be at 4.30 p.m.

The deputation was highly excited, but an almost unnatural calm now descended upon its leader. He held out his wrist to Dr. Schnirer, Vice-President of the Zionist Actions Committee. The physician felt the pulse.

'Hmph! Just 100. Rather high.'

'Not for me,' said Herzl. 'It was that before I received the summons.'

He dressed with meticulous care. He took Wolffsohn with him, and his friend equipped himself with a pocket-brush to make sure that he could valet Herzl at the last moment, if necessary.

They arrived at 4.30 p.m. precisely, but they were not received until two hours later. At 6.15 they heard a fanfare of trumpets, the clatter of hoofs of a royal guard, and officers' sharp commands followed by the clink of presented arms, indicating that the Kaiser had arrived.

A few minutes later Herzl's name was called. As he walked up the broad stairs to the audience chamber he noticed that a smart-looking officer was looking him over out of the corner of his eye, taking in Herzl's well-fitting coat, the impeccable crease to his trousers and his highly polished shoes. As soon as Herzl's name was announced, the officer drew himself stiffly to attention, clicked his heels, held out his hand and introduced himself.

'Count von Kessel.'

Herzl responded, and a smile of pleasure passed over the Count's face. But he was now looking past Herzl, who followed his gaze and saw the Empress and von Bülow. He gestured to Herzl to enter the chamber.

He entered with head bowed respectfully. The Kaiser, who wore the dark uniform of an officer of a Hussar regiment, stepped forward to greet him.

Herzl had the impression that, if not delighted, the Kaiser was certainly interested to meet him.

'All-Highest, I consider myself most fortunate to be granted this opportunity.'

The Kaiser motioned Herzl to a chair and sat down with his back to the writing-table. He stretched out his legs, bright in the polished Hussar boots, and crossed them with the gesture of one who is making ready for a long, intimate chat.

Herzl's journalistic eyes took note of the Kaiser's appearance. He saw a man almost as tall as himself, with curious sea-blue eyes – regal, majestic, infinitely searching and inquiring. Herzl kept his gaze on those eyes, but inwardly he was consumed with nervousness. He hoped the tension would be relieved by some preliminary conversation. But the Kaiser said:

'Please begin.'

'At what point, your Majesty?'

'Wherever you wish,' he answered, a little mockingly it appeared. He leaned back against the table.

Herzl began in an uncertain voice to draw the Kaiser's attention to certain passages in the preliminary letter he had written to him. His heart beat rapidly, yet he was sufficiently self-possessed to note that von Bülow appeared to be deriving some satisfaction from his embarrassment.

The Kaiser explained why he favoured the Zionist idea, and Herzl had to use all his powers of concentration to take in what he was saying and at the same time mentally formulate his replies. His Majesty kept referring to the Jews as Herzl's *Landsleute* (fellow-countrymen) and there was a faint hint of antisemitism in what he said.

'There is no doubt that with all the money at the disposal of the Jews you should be able to carry out your colonisation plans in Palestine,' he suggested. 'There are certain elements among your people whom it would be a good thing to transfer to Palestine. I have in mind Herse, for example, where there are a number of moneylenders. If they betook themselves with their possessions to Palestine they would do very well.'

Herzl burned with inward anger at the suggestion that moneylenders were typical of Jewry, but he concealed his feelings. He gave the Kaiser a short explanatory lecture on antisemitism. This disease injured the best of Jews, he explained.

Von Bülow now intervened to remark that many of the richest and most prominent Jews did not share Herzl's views, and some of the most influential newspapers definitely opposed them.

'I knew I could expect opposition from him,' Herzl reflected, but he would not be drawn. Von Bülow was obviously set on convincing the Kaiser that there was not really much power behind Herzl's views, but he was able to suggest by means of reservations and carefully interposed 'ifs' and 'buts' that he had his serious doubts about the whole business.

However, the Kaiser seemed to be encouraging Herzl with nods, gestures and exclamations. Their talk now switched to general politics. Reference was made to the Dreyfus case and Herzl was astonished to see that the Kaiser and his advisers were completely convinced that Dreyfus was innocent.

Finally, after looking at his watch, His Majesty asked Herzl if he had any further questions. Herzl raised the issue of the reception of the deputation in Palestine.

'Send von Bülow a memorandum,' came the answer. The Kaiser brought up the subject of the Sultan. 'He knows I am probably the only monarch in Europe who supports him. What do you want me to ask of him for your movement?'

'A chartered company under German protection,' Herzl answered immediately.

'Very good. A chartered company.' He gave Herzl a strong handshake and left the room.

At the hotel the delegation was waiting in a fever of expectancy. Herzl gave them only the barest details and then excused himself. His heart was troubling him and he had to work on the memorandum. He wrote on and on until 11 p.m. while Wolffsohn was packing his cases. He refreshed himself with a draught of Bavarian beer and tried to get a few hours' sleep. But at 4 a.m. he was wide awake again. He lit all the twelve candles in his room and worked at the memorandum for another half-hour. Then he dropped utterly exhausted on the bed. He woke up again at 6 a.m. and laboured for two and a half hours, finishing the draft. He sent it off with a covering letter to von Bülow.

Meanwhile the faithful Wolffsohn had attended

to all the details of the journey, and he had only to go down to the harbour and embark.

As soon as he felt the teak planks of the Russian vessel under his feet he was able to relax. For a whole week there was nothing to do but sit and think. The bright sunshine did not prevent his worrying about how the Turks would react to his Palestine visit. When the vessel docked at Smyrna he asked a Syrian journalist colleague to go through the press service cables to see if anything had been transmitted about his interview with the Kaiser. There was not a word.

'Well,' he told Wolffsohn, 'such an important diplomatic event cannot be kept secret for long. We'll see what happens. If this deputation in Jerusalem succeeds, the hardest part of our task will have been accomplished. What follows is only the working out of details. Others can do that.'

He felt again the tremor round his heart and lay back in his deck-chair and relaxed. He recovered well during the rest of the voyage. On October 26, he stood by the rail and gazed at the harbour of Jaffa. At last he was in sight of Palestine. Was it also the Promised Land?

'This is the land of my fathers,' the former assimilated Austrian Jew told himself. 'What strange emotions this modest strip of neglected soil excites in the minds of such different people!' His eyes ranged over some of his fellow-passengers. There was a Baptist pastor from South Africa, a Russian peasant who had travelled by the horrible third-class accommodation, an Arab from Constantinople. There was an old Jewish woman from Rumania hastening anxiously to the bedside of a daughter, lying dangerously ill in Jerusalem. She was desperately worried lest the Turkish port authorities should fail to accept her passport and send her back.

Herzl smiled. 'I think we can arrange something for her,' he thought.

Then, as now, ships disembarking at Jaffa put off their passengers in lighters. Herzl and his party transferred to one belonging to Thomas Cook and Son. He took care to put the old woman in the same boat. He asked another passenger, Mme. Caulis, the wife of a French journalist, to take charge of her and say she was her personal servant. The old woman clutched the lady's skirt and passed the officials successfully. She was overcome with happiness at the thought of seeing her sick daughter.

'Strange what queer interpretations people put on the word "happiness",' said Herzl, and returned to his own worries over the interview with the Kaiser.

The bustling confusion in the port was maddening. The sun was flaming and no carriage was available. As they waited they heard a royal salute of guns, which indicated that the Emperor had just arrived by the land route. Herzl hired a horse and was about to ride off when the faithful Wolffsohn arrived with a carriage. They set out along the hot, dusty road to the Mikveh Israel agricultural school a few miles away.

The gates were gaily bedecked in honour of the

Emperor, who was to pass that way on the morrow.

The head of the school was in a quandary. He was obviously thrilled to see Theodor Herzl, but dared not express his joy too openly lest he should offend Baron Edmond de Rothschild, whose funds supported the institution. The same dilemma faced many of the colonists who had been settled through the Baron's aid. Each was afraid his neighbour might report him to Rothschild's officials for showing too much joy at Herzl's arrival.

Herzl inspected the wine cellars at Rishon le-Zion. They were the second largest in the world. He remarked to Wolffsohn: "It is not startling to see an industry like this. With enough capital it is possible to set up any enterprise. What upsets me is the thought of the millions that have been poured out and wasted here through sloth, negligence and peculation. Think what good they could have been made to do.'

News of Herzl's coming had preceded him. Crowds lined the route wherever he went, but he was not carried away by their enthusiasm. They tried to hail him as a leader and deliverer, but their speeches were strangely cautious. They obviously had to make diplomatic remarks in which praise of Herzl's efforts was balanced with tributes to the Baron.

'The Baron and I,' Herzl would say in reply, 'have different aims; but I can see that your gratitude to him must be beyond measure, and rightly so.'

He saw a good deal. He noted the contrast between the spacious and comfortable homes of the successful planters and the hovels in which their underpaid workmen lived. Dr. Maze, the medical officer, told him malaria was their main menace and could only be fought by extensive projects designed to drain the swamps. In between these journeys he found time to finish the Zionist deputation's address to the Kaiser and send it to his officials.

At the Jewish village of Wadi El Hanin the whole population turned out to greet him and the children sang. An old man gave him some bread, salt, and wine which he had won from his own soil. Herzl had to enter every home. As they journeyed on a band of young men on horseback came storming towards him, firing rifles and shouting *Hedad* and 'Hoch, Herzl!' (Hurrah, Herzl). The eyes of the deputation filled with tears at the sight of these free, hard-riding young men.

At Rehovot the excitement mounted even higher. This colony was not dependent on the Baron. The inhabitants turned out solidly to welcome their leader.

That concluded the exhausting day and they returned to Jaffa. Herzl was so tired that he could hardly stand upright. The constant strain of meeting people and his heart weakness almost overcame him. He got as much rest as he could that night. Next day the group again went to Mikveh Israel, where he hoped to have a word with the Kaiser as he passed through on his way to Jerusalem.

As the Kaiser came into sight Herzl gave a signal,

and the children burst into the German anthem, *Heil dir im Siegerkranz.* Herzl solemnly removed his sun helmet and the Kaiser recognised him. He reined in his horse at Herzl's side. Herzl took two steps towards him and His Majesty bent down over his horse's neck and offered his hand. Herzl stood bareheaded.

'How are you?' the Kaiser asked.

'I thank your Majesty. I am touring the country. How has your Majesty enjoyed your trip so far?'

'It is very hot. But this land has a future.'

'But now it is a sick country,' said Herzl.

'It needs water, much water.'

'Yes, your Majesty, canalisation and irrigation on a vast scale.'

'The land has a future,' the Kaiser repeated. He shook Herzl's hand again and rode on his way.

Wolffsohn had been very busy with his camera and had exposed two plates.

'I wouldn't part with these,' he exclaimed proudly, 'for ten thousand marks.'

But unfortunately, when the photographer at Jaffa came to develop the pictures he found that one plate showed only the Kaiser's shadow and his left leg, while the other was a complete blank.

CHAPTER TEN

The Search for the Charter

THE next day, a Friday, the party set off by train for Jerusalem. Herzl felt slightly feverish. He must have suffered slight heatstroke while waiting bareheaded for the Emperor at Mikveh Israel. The train was delayed and pulled into Jerusalem station well after the Sabbath had begun. Wolffsohn was very distressed. He did not want Herzl to walk, and yet if he rode through Jerusalem on the Sabbath he would give grave offence to the Orthodox Jews.

Herzl decided to undertake the thirty-minute walk. He leaned heavily on a stick and his friends supported him. When they reached the hotel he was completely spent. He had an attack of vomiting and lay down utterly exhausted. Wolffsohn reproached himself bitterly, convinced that Herzl's last hour had come. Dr. Schnirer massaged the sick man's body with oil of camphor and insisted on spending the night in his room. By morning the patient had made a fair recovery.

Herzl did not form too happy an impression of Jerusalem; the dirt, squalor and poverty upset him, especially in the Jewish quarter of the Old City. 'How I long for the day when Jerusalem will be ours; we shall make it our first task to clean up this city,' he said. 'A bright new Jerusalem will arise in place of this centuries-old squalor.'

The Turks had gone to extraordinary pains to welcome the Emperor to Jerusalem. When it was calculated that he could not pass on horseback through one of the city gates because of the height of his plumed helmet, they tore down part of the wall. They erected a triumphal arch for him and the Jewish population did likewise. Herzl had planned to deliver an address of welcome under the arch, but the rabbis and communal leaders, fearing the reactions of the Turkish authorities, persuaded him to abandon the attempt.

Herzl was worried about the deputation. There were indications that they might not be received after all, and the clearly hostile attitude of the local Turkish officials and the German diplomats and Consular officials strengthened these fears. The councillor of the Legation had made cuts in Herzl's address to the Emperor. Some of the passages he deleted referred to Zionist aims and asked His Majesty's protection for the proposed Jewish land company in Palestine.

How was he to cut the diplomatic red-tape and remind the Emperor of his existence? He had a brainwave; he would prepare an album of the Jewish colonies in Palestine and ask His Majesty to accept it. But this manoeuvre proved unnecessary.

On November 2, he was received by the Emperor. He read his address, stressing that Palestine was the historic home of Jewry, that it was crying out for cultivation, that there were Jews throughout the world who needed land. Could not the two be brought together?

'We must investigate this further,' His Majesty said. 'There is room here for everyone. . . . The main need is water. . . It will cost millions. . . .'

'Billions,' Herzl corrected him. 'We shall find them. After all, the money will create billions of new wealth.'

Von Bülow sneered: 'When money is in question your people have far less of a problem getting hold of it than we have.'

There was some more talk, but the interview was very short. Herzl felt decidedly disturbed as he left the audience chamber. He stopped for a moment to speak to Count von Kessel.

'Finished so soon?' the officer asked. Herzl thought he detected some diminution in the cordiality he had been shown in Constantinople. It confirmed his impression that the anti-Zionist forces in the German Chancellery had been hard at work.

'Well,' he comforted himself. 'He didn't say yes and he didn't say no.' Now he wanted to get away with his friends as quickly as possible. For a while the police delayed him. Out of the corner of his eye he caught sight of Mendel Kramer, the Turkish secret police agent who had been dogging his steps ever since he landed in Palestine.

'We had better depart as unobtrusively as possible,' Herzl told his companions. 'We'll pack our bags quietly tonight and take the first train out at dawn.'

During his brief tour of Jerusalem, Herzl had been impressed by David's tower. Now, fearing arrest, he told his friends: 'It would be most appropriate if they imprisoned me in King David's fortress.'

As soon as the train reached Jaffa they hastened to the port, but no ship was leaving. They passed an anxious day and then hired a boat which took them out to a large steamer lying in the roadstead. It was calling at Beirut. As this town, too, was Turkish territory, it was useless to them. They asked Gordon Bennett, of the 'New York Herald', whose yacht was lying in the harbour, to take them, but he was not leaving for some days. Finally, they obtained a vessel of the Prince Line leaving next day. They reached Alexandria two days later and transhipped to a larger steamer.

The next task was to discover the result of the interview. The German officials had told Herzl that the Emperor would make his views known in an official communiqué. It was not till they reached Naples that they saw it. At the end of a dull Court chronicle of His Majesty's movements, came the following:

'JERUSALEM, November 2. . . . later the Emperor received a Jewish deputation which presented him with an album of pictures of the Jewish colonies in Palestine. In response to an address by the leader of the delegation, His Majesty stated that he looked benevolently on all efforts to improve agriculture in Palestine so long as these were in the best interests of the Turkish Empire and were conducted in a spirit of absolute respect for the Sultan's sovereignty.'

Not a word about a charter, a land company or protection of special Jewish interests. The opposition had triumphed. The deputation left the vessel in a pessimistic mood. Even the faithful and always cheerful Wolffsohn was downcast. Herzl realised that it was his duty to put a good face on things and cheer up his companions. He said to them: 'Now you see why I must be your leader. I am neither wiser nor better than any of you. But in this crisis I can know no yielding. That is why I am a leader. Even in worse moments than this I never let go but prepare for greater sacrifices.'

He reasoned that the failure with the Emperor might even turn out for the best. His Imperial Majesty's patronage for a Jewish State might be good short-term policy, but in the long run the price of involving the Jewish State in the Turkish-German European imbroglio might prove too high.

He was a true prophet. If Germany had held a protectorate over a Jewish State in Palestine it would have been overwhelmed in the Kaiser's, and Turkey's downfall at the close of the 1914-18 war. As it happened, it was during that war, on November 2, 1917, exactly 19 years to the day after Herzl had last spoken with the Kaiser, that the British Government issued the Balfour Declaration proclaiming to the world that 'His Majesty's Government view with favour the establishment in Palestine of a national home for the Jewish people.'

Moreover, the very fact that the Emperor received Herzl in his capacity as President of the World Zionist Organisation was of supreme political importance. The Imperial communiqué was meaningless, but the diplomatic world now knew that the Jewish people had an organisation working to regain Jewish statehood. Jewry had an address, that of the World Zionist Organisation which Herzl had called into being.

Meanwhile a storm of criticism broke over his head. His opponents rejoiced in his failure, and even in his Zionist movement there were many who said he had promised more than he could perform. He held his peace. The documents that could have cleared him must be kept secret in order to make future negotiations smoother. His state of health left him no strength for empty arguments. The thing to do was to press on as fast as possible; who knew how much time he had left?

In all these troubles his sense of humour did not desert him. In his diary he recorded a jest current in Vienna. The Emperor was supposed to have said: 'This Zionism is a wonderful thing. What a pity it has to be carried out by Jews.'

The Third Congress was to be held in the summer of 1899 and Herzl wished to have the Bank finally organised before it met. It had been duly registered in London in March under the name of the Jewish Colonial Trust. But subscriptions came in slowly, and it was only in July that the sum of £250,000 which it required to open its doors was finally obtained.

Herzl pushed on with his political activity on every possible front. On May 18, 1899, at a conference to consider universal peace convened at The Hague, in Holland, Herzl engaged a well-known pacifist, Baroness Bertha von Suttner, to move among the diplomats gathered there and try to win support for the aims of Zionism. He himself arrived in the middle of June to help in the effort.

Among the less reputable characters he met was one Nouri Bey, of the Turkish Foreign Office. Herzl was looking for someone to take the place of Count Nevlinski, who had died suddenly a few months previously. He had no option but to make use of this man Nouri in order to maintain contact with the Sultan's Court.

One evening he dined privately with Nouri Bey in his suite. Nouri asked Herzl what his exact aims were and what he intended requesting the Sultan if he ever managed to see him.

'I wanted a chartered company,' Herzl said.

'Can you get the Kaiser's support for this?'

'Definitely.'

'Then it might be done,' Nouri declared. 'But you must have a consortium. There are a lot of men in key positions in Constantinople who are just waiting to be bribed. I can fix it for you. I know who'll bring it in. I know the price of every man. I play fair with them and they know it. By the way,' he added with an oily smile, 'you will have to bribe me as well.'

Herzl felt a shudder of distaste as he looked at this unpleasant, shifty character. But had no option. He must replace his former agent, Nevlinski.

'So if we have this consortium, what are the prospects?' he asked.

'With the consortium and the Emperor's help it can be done.'

An entirely different personality was the Russian State Councillor, Ivan Bloch, whom Herzl won to support of Zionism at this peace conference. Bloch was a man of the highest calibre; indeed, this peace conference initiated by Nicholas II had originally been his idea. He promised to do what he could to arrange an interview between Herzl and the Tsar.

Herzl made a round of the capitals of Europe in the interests of the Bank and in preparation for the Third Zionist Congress, which was held at Basle in the middle of August, 1899. In his opening speech he called attention to the inauguration of the Bank. He reported the fact of his interview with the Emperor, but did not discuss it beyond stressing its implications for the prestige of the movement.

The Congress went fairly smoothly and Herzl's health did not suffer. At this stage his greatest anxiety was in regard to his position on the 'Neue Freie Presse', which was hostile and did not allow him to write what he wished. He longed to be able to give up the 'few thousand filthy gulden' he got from the paper, but he had to support his family. His savings had long since been engulfed in 'Die Welt'.

He tried to write plays and earn some money by free-lance work, and this ate into the scanty leisure he had for his family and children. It was a sad and unhappy time, and the pressure of the diplomatic struggle in which he was engaged became greater month by month. Through Hechler he tried to see the Prince of Wales. He had good friends working to bring about his interview with the Tsar; at Constantinople, his consortium, he hoped, was industriously working to achieve an audience of the Sultan for him.

Inside the World Zionist Organisation discontent was increasing. There was disagreement with his handling of the Bank's operations, and for a while even his relations with Wolffsohn were strained. Some wanted more time spent on cultural affairs. Money was difficult to come by as the sums required for diplomacy had to be found and spent in secrecy. But his character toughened and developed to meet the crisis. He was sufficiently sensitive to divine the motives, fears and desires of others. He was dictatorial enough to keep a tight hold on the reins of policy and ensure that the movement did not lose direction because of the differing viewpoints of his colleagues. He was sufficiently inspired and dedicated to be able to infuse others with his own high ideals, courage and determination.

At this time, too, circumstances in Eastern Europe combined to arouse the opposition to fever-heat. The Jews of Rumania were caught up in a wave of virulent antisemitism. There had been bad harvests the previous year and, following their standard technique, the authorities diverted the minds of the people from the real cause of their troubles by inciting them against the Jews. The result was a desperate Jewish emigration. Herzl's enemies suggested that it was his Zionist advocacy of mass emigration that had put it into the minds of the Jews to flee. Many of the refugees did swamp Herzl with requests for aid. Poor people besieged his house and this estranged his wife even more, for with her wealthy upbringing she found it difficult to endure these hungry, ragged supplicants for her husband's assistance. She did not realise that his name had become a symbol of hope for all needy, hopeless, desperate Jews. Herzl did what he could to persuade the authorities of every land to grant the refugees asylum.

The Fourth Congress, to be held in London, now occupied much of his thought. Some instinct, added to his shrewd knowledge of affairs, told him that Britain might well prove a decisive factor in rebuilding the Jewish nation. He did not live to see how right he was. What he hoped for was that the close contact with the Zionist movement which a Congress in London would give the British public might bring Her Majesty's ministers and the great Jewish leaders of England to a clearer understanding of the aims of Zionism.

In his opening speech to the Congress on August 13, 1900, Herzl made an impassioned plea to British public opinion.

'England, great England, freedom-loving England, surveying all the seas, will understand our movement. From here the idea of Zionism will soar higher and higher . . . . We are but the bearers of a banner which, in other hands, will some day fly, we hope, over a happy Israel.'

The publicity which followed the London Congress was favourable on the whole. A general election was to be held and the English Zionist Federation canvassed the candidates. A great number promised that if they were elected they would support the aims of Zionism.

The round of political negotiations was resumed, with Herzl still seeking his interview with the Sultan. He also tried to interest a bankers' consortium concerning the Turkish national debt so that he could have a strong backing if he ever got to the stage of actual negotiations for the Palestine Charter.

At home he was having greater difficulties than ever with the 'Neue Freie Presse'. In his diary on May 2, 1900, he wrote sadly:

> This is my fortieth birthday.
> The wind blows through the short mown grass,
> My steps must twice as quickly pass.

'It is six years since I began this movement which has left me old, weary and impoverished.'

To add to his troubles reports came from Russia that the Zionists there were deeply disappointed with the London Congress and were not inclined to attend another if it should prove to be so 'lacking in content'. The news depressed him.

'If they really keep away,' he said, 'our next meeting at Basle will not draw more than eighty delegates and will be a demonstration only of the waning strength of our movement.' He went on: 'It seems to me that sixty rather than six years have passed since I began all this by writing "Judenstaat".'

CHAPTER ELEVEN

Herzl and Abdul Hamid

NOURI BEY and his consortium took Herzl's money but did little or nothing to help him obtain his interview with the Sultan Abdul Hamid II, ruler of the Ottoman Empire. Herzl was convinced that if he spoke personally to the Sultan he could persuade him that it would be in Turkey's interests to allow the Jews to populate and, as a subject State develop the neglected strip of land south of Syria. In exchange, he was confident that he could muster sufficient funds to make a substantial contribution towards getting Abdul Hamid out of the financial difficulties which were ruining him and his empire.

Watching Abdul Hamid's struggles to retain his position were the great Powers of the world. Russia had a long history of ambition in the Middle East. She was determined to dominate the passage through the Dardanelles, which Turkey controlled, and to obtain an outlet into the Mediterranean. It was to her advantage to see the Sultan fall. Britain, with her stake in Egypt, did not want a strong Turkey. France would not be grief-stricken should any disaster happen to the Ottoman Empire, for she, too, had her interests in the Levant and wanted to push them further. Germany, who hungrily sought a place in the sun, saw that this might be best obtained by posing as Turkey's great friend and supporter against her waiting, watchful circle of enemies. This explains why Herzl began his approach to the Sultan through the Kaiser, for anything the Emperor told Abdul Hamid would have great weight.

Herzl knew enough about the international situation to be aware that Abdul Hamid was trying to use Germany for his own ends and would do the same with him. But he felt that all the risks were outweighed by the importance of gaining a foothold for a national settlement in Palestine. Once that was obtained the Zionist Organisation, with himself at the head, would have to try to find its own way through the shifting sands of Middle Eastern diplomacy. The main thing was to obtain some sort of reasonable Charter and to begin to build the Jewish State.

These policies were beginning to meet with organised opposition inside the World Zionist Organisation. This was revealed clearly at the Fifth Congress held in Basle on December 26, 1901. The Zionists of Eastern Europe set up the first political party in Zionism. They called themselves the Democratic Zionist Fraction, and their aim was a programme of practical colonisation in Palestine irrespective of the political aspect. They also wanted a world-wide drive to spread the Zionist idea among the Jewish people, especially the youth. Among those who headed this group was Chaim Weizmann, who called for a properly worked out programme of Jewish-nationalist cultural activity.

At this Congress too, the Jewish National Fund, originally suggested by Professor Hermann Schapira at the First Congress, was instituted. This was to be a world-wide body devoted to raising funds, even in the smallest sums – 'A penny a day is the J.N.F. way' – from the whole of Jewry. These pennies, Schapira claimed, would aggregate to large sums and would be used to purchase land in Palestine upon which to settle those who were prepared to work it themselves. Such land was not to be used, like that of the Rothschild colonies, for plantation-owners to work by hired labour. The worker of a J.N.F. plot held it for 49 years, according to the Biblical law, after which it went back to the J.N.F., but the lease could of course be renewed. The idea was to ensure Jewish labour on this land, which would not be subject to exploitation or speculation, but remain for ever 'the inalienable property of all the Jewish people'.

Herzl did not realise, nor did many others at the time, that the resolution bringing the Jewish National Fund into being was one of the most important practical steps taken by the World Zionist Organisation towards the re-establishment of the State of Israel. The purchase of land began a few years later. Thenceforth during the next four decades the Fund acquired territory from Turkish and Arab owners by straightforward purchase at the market value. Whenever there were Arab tenants, the Fund paid them compensation which enabled them to start a new life elsewhere, although this was not strictly required by law in all cases. The Zionist Organisation also had a strategic plan for buying land, so that the holdings would cover an area of Palestine which could, when the time came, form a State.

Politically this was of the utmost importance. Whenever, in later times, the British wished to bring the National Home experiment to an end or curtail it drastically, they were faced with a fact – Jews were already living as a national group on a considerable portion of Palestine's territory. They could no longer be written off by a political or diplomatic decision. When later on the United Nations had to tackle the problem of what to do with the Jews and Arabs of Palestine, they sent a commission of inquiry to look into the situation. They found that the Jews, settled on Jewish National Fund land, with factories, schools, hospitals, a university, industries, theatres, farms and homes, colonies and settlements, looked so much like a State already that they decided to set up separate Jewish and Arab States.

Before this vital Fifth Congress took place, Herzl realised his desire to have an audience of Sultan Abdul Hamid II. Nouri Bey's consortium had little to do with the arrangement. Herzl had made friends with Arminius Vambery, a former explorer and political agent for both the British and the Turks. He was now peacefully occupying the Chair of Oriental Languages at Budapest University. He had once been tutor to Abdul Hamid's sister. It was he who arranged the interview.

Long and complicated were the intrigues, abundant the bribes, and nerve-racking the suspense before the morning of Friday, May 18, 1901 arrived, and Herzl waited in the ante-room to the Sultan's audience chamber. Just before he was admitted to the presence, the Master of Ceremonies informed him that His Majesty was graciously bestowing upon him the Order of the Medidje, Second Class. Fearful though he was that this might at the last moment wreck the long-awaited audience, Herzl said that he could not, in his position, accept Second Class. The official went out and, after an interval full of suspense for Herzl, came back, wreathed in smiles, with the First Class of the Order.

Shortly afterwards, he was ushered into the presence. He looked at the Sultan. 'This man is the source of all my hopes and anxieties,' he told himself. 'He is either a symbol or the unconscious tool of all these gangs of fools, thieves and rogues who have gathered round him and who, by their greed and stupid maladministration, are bringing this Empire down to ruin.'

He saw before him a thin man of small stature, with a sallow face framed by a full beard dyed red. His nose was prominent and crooked and he had yellow, broken teeth. When he spoke his voice was reedy and tremulous, but these physical defects were compensated by the blaze and glory of his official robes.

Abdul Hamid extended his hand to Herzl and motioned him to be seated in a comfortable armchair. He reclined on his divan, with his scimitar gleaming wickedly between his knees. Beside him stood Ibrahim Bey, agile and nervous, who was to act as interpreter, and who leaped from one to the other as each spoke.

The Sultan studiously avoided any mention of the Zionist movement or Herzl's connection with it. He maintained the fiction that he was granting an interview to the correspondent of the 'Neue Freie Presse'. Thus a good deal of the first part of the talk, which lasted two hours, was taken up with general politics and Herzl's delicate but ingenious attempts to steer the conversation into the channel he wished it to take – the grant of a Charter for Jewish settlement in Palestine. At last he found an opening.

'I hear with great delight that Your Majesty is a good friend of the Jews. I have long sought an opportunity to render Your Majesty any assistance in my power.'

Thus, without formally abandoning the fiction that he was only a newspaperman, Herzl spoke as the head of a powerful, representative, Jewish organisation would express himself; for what business had a correspondent of the 'Neue Freie Presse' to convey such sentiments on behalf of the Jewish people?

The Sultan drew out a delicately chased silver cigarette case, extracted two cigarettes, put one in his own mouth and gave one to Herzl. Ibrahim Bey quickly provided a light.

'I always have been, and am now, a friend of the Jews. I rely almost entirely on Moslems and Jews. I have not such confidence in my other citizens,' the Sultan answered.

Herzl seized the opportunity to dilate on the cruelty shown to Jews in other parts of the world.

'Not in my dominions,' boasted the Sultan. 'The gates of my Empire are wide open to Jewish refugees.'

Herzl then tried warily to refer to the Sultan's finances, so that he could bring up the matter of the Charter.

'Your Majesty must have heard the story of Androcles and the Lion. I would like to be your Androcles and extract a certain thorn from your paw. May I speak frankly?'

Sighing deeply, the Sultan beckoned to him to continue.

'The matter must remain a deep secret,' Herzl cautioned.

Abdul Hamid cast his eyes piously heavenward, placed one hand on his heart and murmured, 'Secret, secret!'

Herzl continued: 'I am anxious to win for Your Majesty the undying affection of all Jews throughout the world. This will require from Your Majesty an important manifesto. Your Empire lacks but one thing, the stimulus to industry, which my people could give. When Europeans come to Turkey they grow wealthy very quickly and return to Europe with their spoils. I can understand people coming with the idea of getting wealth; but surely they ought to stay in the land that gives them the opportunity to gather riches?'

The Sultan nodded vigorously and said: 'My Empire has untold sources of wealth. Only today I received a telegram from Baghdad stating that oil has been discovered, gushing with a flow that makes the oil fields of the Caucasus seem a trickle. Look at my iron deposits, my seams of gold and silver. In the old days my predecessors used to take bars of solid gold out of the bowels of the earth, stamp them with their seal and pay their soldiers wages with them!'

The discussion ranged over the whole field of Government finances; now Herzl began to realise what the Sultan was after. Abdul Hamid was trying to discover how he could use him. Herzl took the plunge.

'I would like to ask Your Majesty three things; but they must be secret.'

'Secret, secret!' the ruler breathed with pious emphasis.

'I would like a copy of Your Majesty's plan for repaying the debt,' Herzl said, referring to one of the subjects they had already mentioned. 'And I would like Your Majesty to consider the necessity to issue a proclamation favourable to Jews, giving them your protection and assuring them asylum in your dominions.'

This concluded the interview. The Sultan had only nodded vigorously without committing himself. As Herzl left the Palace he was besieged by eager hands seeking 'baksheesh', which he distributed lavishly.

The next morning he was again summoned to the Palace. He sat down to a meal with some of the high Court officials, who handed him a diamond tie-pin, a gift from the Sultan. Not till later did he discover that its stones were of poor quality. They left him in no doubt of the Sultan's intentions. He intended to use Herzl as a tool in a shady market operation. A syndicate was to be organised to buy up Turkish Government bonds, which had fallen to a quarter of their value. In this way the Sultan would cheat his creditors and get free of his debts.

'The dirty thieves,' Herzl thought. 'I must have time to think it over,' he told them tactfully. Realising that he was not to have an audience of the Sultan, he took his leave.

The next few days were occupied with tortuous and tough negotiations. The Turks were trying to inveigle Herzl into their schemes and he, in turn, was trying to find some honest means by which he could serve the Sultan. At the end of the negotiations he found he had been enticed into undertaking to prove the seriousness of his pretensions by making available the sum of £1,500,000. He was also told Turkey's conditions for Jewish immigration: Jews must renounce their previous citizenship and become

Turkish subjects; they would be liable for military duty; they would not be allowed to emigrate to Palestine wholesale but only in small groups of a few families at a time; they would not be settled in a continuous stretch of territory.

Herzl tactfully rejected these conditions and renewed his plea for the Jews to be allowed free settlement in Palestine, which was, for the most part, desolate, unpopulated and neglected. He comforted himself with the thought that the outcome was not entirely negative. They had at least begun negotiations. In fact he never got any closer than this to the Charter, but he had fitted one more rung in the ladder which led to the Balfour Declaration of 1917, the League of Nations Mandate of 1922, and the United Nations decision of 1947 to set up a Jewish State. If he could have known this he would have been comforted, but he did know he had made the return of the Jews to Palestine an integral element in the Middle Eastern problem.

'This is the beginning of real and practical negotiations,' he told his colleagues. 'All we need now is luck, diplomacy and the necessary finance.'

The diplomacy was there, but the luck and the money were not. The Jewish bankers refused to help. The Sultan's advisers were pressing for payment of the £1,500,000 and the entire capital of the Zionist Bank was only £250,000. Herzl persisted in his efforts and, after negotiating throughout February, 1902, for the Charter, he did receive an offer of land in Asia Minor, which he refused. In July, 1902, at the Sultan's request, he went back to Constantinople and received from the Court Treasurer a bag of gold to cover his expenses. It was now obvious that he had been used as a decoy to further the Sultan's intrigue with the bankers whom he was trying to persuade to pay his debts. Without financial backing the Zionists would gain nothing from Herzl's diplomacy, however brilliant it was. The opportunity passed, never to return.

CHAPTER TWELVE

Rothschild and Chamberlain

ZIONISM was now taken seriously by the Great Powers. They realised that in discussions on the Middle East it must be reckoned as an instrument which they might be able to use. So when an opportunity arose for Herzl to interest Britain in his schemes, he found her receptive.

In the summer of 1902 he was invited to appear before a Royal Commission of the British Parliament which was investigating the subject of immigration into the British Isles from Eastern Europe. Only 30,000 Jews had fled from Tsarist Russia to England, but this influx had been enough to start a public outcry. People claimed that they threatened the labour market. Now the Commission was examining the facts and was to recommend how many penniless immigrants, which meant mainly Jews, were to be allowed to enter the British Isles.

Herzl journeyed to London from Berlin. No sooner had he arrived than he was summoned back by news from Vienna that his father was dying. He hurried to his beloved parent's death-bed; but he had no time for grief. He returned to London to appear before the Royal Commission.

At that time Lord Rothschild was head of the Anglo-Jewish community. He was a member of the Royal Commission and was furious when he heard that the British Zionists had arranged for Herzl to appear before it and give evidence. He was afraid he would tell the members all about Zionism and so make them feel doubtful about the complete identification of the Jews with Britain and thus uncertain as to their citizenship. Herzl had for years been hammering at the Rothschilds for a chance to discuss his plans thoroughly. Now at last Rothschild determined to talk matters over with him. He fixed an interview with the Zionist leader.

Herzl arranged his journey so as to be at New Court, St. Swithin's Lane, the Rothschild headquarters, exactly on time. To be late would be a discourtesy, to be early might be taken as over-anxiety on his part. He was at once shown into Rothschild's presence. The banker began the discussion immediately. He was hard of hearing and, like many deaf people, did not know how loud he was talking. Herzl felt that he was being bullied and began to shout back. Rothschild attacked the ideas of Zionism and started to lay down the law on what Herzl should and should not say to the Commission.

Herzl was not in the easiest of moods. His health was bad, his father's recent death weighed heavily on his spirits, and he was fully aware that it was the opposition of the House of Rothschild which had made it so hard to get the Jewish Colonial Trust Bank started.

After several attempts he managed to interrupt Rothschild's outburst to say briefly and pointedly, 'I shall do what I have always done. I shall tell the Commission what I think is right and what my conscience dictates.'

Referring to Rothschild's anti-Zionist remarks, he went on: 'It is not true that all the Governments are united in opposing my ideas. I have dealt directly with Germany and Russia and they view my aims favourably. I am of the opinion that Britain, also, will not oppose them. I am on good terms with your Government.'

'You are received everywhere because you are Herzl of the "Neue Freie Presse". Do not deceive yourself,' shouted Rothschild.

'Nonsense,' Herzl rejoined heatedly. 'My publishers are deadly enemies of my plans. To this very day the word Zionism is forbidden in that paper.'

After more argument Herzl realised that Rothschild was shrewdly probing for his weak spots. The banker suddenly said:

'They are summoning you to the Commission as a witness, as one of the foremost Jews in the world. They expect you to tell them that no Jew can really become an Englishman.'

'Do you think I would be so arrogant as to presume to lecture this Commission on what is, and what is not, a true Englishman? All I intend to do is tell them simply of the terrible conditions in which the Jews of East Europe are living. Those people must either get out or perish. There are 700,000 such victims in Galicia alone.'

'For God's sake,' Rothschild exclaimed, 'don't tell the Commission that. They'll imagine all the 700,000 will make for England. They'll stop all immigration.'

'I shall certainly tell them. You can rely on that.'

Rothschild's jaw dropped. He banged a bell and summoned his brother, Leopold.

'I'm sorry to note that in London Jewish philanthropy seems to have become an instrument fashioned to keep Jews in their misery,' Herzl said sarcastically.

'My God!' wailed Rothschild. 'He's going to tell all this to the Commission.'

'I should be a villain,' Herzl retorted, 'if I said words designed only to limit immigration. But,' he added, 'Anglo-Jewry ought then to set up a statue to me in gratitude for saving them from a mass influx of Jews whose coming might cause antisemitism. However, unfortunately, I have a plan for rescuing those Jews, and that plan I shall put before the Commission.'

At this point Lord Rothschild broke off the discussion and suggested lunch. Several younger members of the Rothschild family joined them for the meal, and Herzl was struck by their close family resemblance.

The break allowed passions to cool down, and

when they had drunk their coffee Herzl went up to Rothschild and asked: 'Would you care to hear my plan now?'

'Yes,' said his lordship meekly enough. He cupped his good ear and inclined his head to Herzl. It was a moment of triumph for the Zionist leader. For over six years he had been trying to get the family to give him a hearing, and now his chance had come.

'I intend to ask the British Government for a Charter of colonisation,' he began.

'Don't use the word Charter,' Lord Rothschild interjected. 'It has unhappy associations here.'

'Call it what you will. I wish to found a Jewish colony on British soil.'

'Would you take Uganda?' inquired Rothschild.

'No! I would accept one of the following places.' As there were others in the room, he took a scrap of notepaper and wrote some names. He handed it to Rothschild, who read it carefully. On the paper was written: THE SINAI PENINSULA, THE EGYPTIAN PORTION OF PALESTINE, CYPRUS.

'Do you agree?' Herzl pressed him.

'Absolutely.'

Herzl appeared before the Royal Commission, but he felt that he made a poor impression. He was over-anxious and excited, and his English, never good, was much more broken than usual. The next day he met Lord James of Hereford, the Chairman, and conveyed what he had really wanted to say. He was told he would have to get the help of the Rothschilds for his colony plan, as Britain could make no funds available. He asked that if an offer was made it should be couched in terms which would attract others than the poorest Jews to the colony.

The next day he met Rothschild again. After they had gone into the plan in great detail Rothschild said: 'Put it down on paper for me. I'll speak to Chamberlain about it on Friday. But I have not the slightest intention of going in for a large scheme. The limit should be 25,000 people.'

'And I have no intention of going in for a small scheme,' replied Herzl.

They ended a long discussion, during which the two men began to know and appreciate each other, with the understanding that Herzl would supply a memorandum. On the British side the proposals developed slowly. It was not until October 22, 1902, that Herzl at last saw Joseph Chamberlain, the Colonial Secretary.

He told Chamberlain that he was negotiating with the Sultan for a Charter in Palestine, but that his people were in too great distress to wait through the long, involved deliberations with an Oriental potentate. They had to find a place of asylum at once. After discussing the possibilities of Cyprus, Chamberlain referred Herzl to the Foreign Secretary, Lord Lansdowne, concerning El Arish in the Sinai Peninsula, and the Egyptian portion of Palestine. They came under his Department. Later, Herzl saw Rothschild again. The great banker was now won over to Herzl personally even if he did not entirely endorse his aims. He said that if the Charter conditions were favourable he would try to assist him in raising the £15,000,000 required, of which £3,000,000 might come from the funds of the Jewish Colonisation Association.

Herzl now had to go to Egypt to finalise negotiations which Leopold Greenberg, the British Zionist leader had been conducting on the Organisation's behalf with the Khedive [ruler] of that country. Meanwhile, an expedition, headed by Leopold Kessler, had been sent to explore the territory round El Arish. It reported that conditions were unfavourable for European settlement and the scarcity of water might prove an insuperable obstacle.

The Khedive decided against a Charter and opposition was growing to any alternative plan. In the end the Egyptian Government stated flatly that no water could be diverted from the Nile for the project and so the whole proposal was dropped.

While these negotiations were continuing, Herzl went back to London and, on April 23, 1903, had another interview with Joseph Chamberlain, who had just come back from a tour of Africa.

He felt weary and deeply depressed as he sat facing the British Colonial Secretary. He had not got over the death of his father, and his bereavement led to gloomy thoughts about himself, for he knew that his heart was getting much worse. The intervals when he was without pain or excessive fatigue were now shorter. For the past seven years the Zionist cause had drained his strength. For it he had sacrificed his family life.

As he looked at Chamberlain he thought: 'This

is my last chance. El Arish is rapidly fading into limbo. The only chance of rescuing it is for the Minister to persuade the Khedive to reconsider the matter. Perhaps he can prevail on that country, which is, after all, a British protectorate, to give us a territory which will at least be contiguous with the borders of the ancient Jewish homeland of Palestine.'

It would have to come soon, very soon. He had not much time left. His personal ambitions with regard to the Jewish State had now been reduced to one grim desire. Let it be established in time for him to be buried within its borders. A short time before the interview he had drawn up his last will and testament. In it he stated: 'I wish to be buried in a grave beside my father, there to rest until the Jewish people shall take me to Palestine.'

Chamberlain seemed tired and harassed by cares of State, but he greeted Herzl with the warmth of an old friend. 'Since we last met,' he said, 'I have seen quite a bit of the world. When I was in Egypt I spoke to Lord Cromer about your affair.'

Herzl explained what had happened to the negotiations. He said El Arish was a very poor territory, but he hoped they could make it do.

'When I was in East Africa,' said Chamberlain. 'I saw a tract of land that would suit you admirably. It is Uganda. It is infernally hot near the coast, but further inland the climate is suitable for Europeans. You could grow sugar and cotton. I thought as I looked at it: "There's a fine piece of land for Dr.

Herzl. What a pity he wants nothing but Palestine or some land close to it".'

Herzl agreed and said that Uganda might well follow, but Palestine had to come first. Chamberlain talked at length about the Middle East and said the time would soon come for the showdown between British, French, Russian and German interests there. Herzl mentally wondered what the position of a new Jewish State would be in such a case. Aloud he stressed that a Jewish buffer State at El Arish might serve British interests. He felt he had impressed Chamberlain.

They talked about the immigration problem, and it appeared that Chamberlain was in favour of the liberal admission of aliens. As he escorted Herzl to the door he promised to speak to Lord Cromer, the British representative in Egypt, about the Egyptian negotiations.

However, the talks with Egypt over El Arish collapsed as had those with the Kaiser and the Sultan. All that was left was Uganda. Herzl laboured to secure a clear commitment on this territory which he could put before the forthcoming Sixth Zionist Congress. The need was desperate. The world had been shaken by terrible news from Tsarist Russia. A pogrom had taken place in Kishinev, in Bessarabia, which exceeded anything in memory for unbridled, murderous savagery. During Easter Week a mob, incited and protected by Tsarist officials, had systematically plundered the Jewish community of that town. It had looted the homes, attacked the women, desecrated the synagogues and beaten and tortured those it did not kill. Of the town's Jewish inhabitants 45 were butchered and 600 were wounded; 1,500 homes were destroyed.

Herzl frantically sought an interview with the Tsar or his ministers to see if he could do something to alleviate the sufferings of the Jews in Russia. He determined to press the Congress to accept the Uganda plan so as to give the tortured Jewish masses at least a temporary refuge during the dark night of waiting until they secured the Jewish State.

As soon as he had obtained a satisfactory assurance on Uganda, he set out for Russia. He was received by the Minister Plehve, who assured him the Tsar would render Zionism moral and material assistance if he could promise that it would lead to a substantial diminution of the Jewish population of Russia. If the negotiations with the Tsar's Ministers meant little, the reception he received from the Jewish masses wherever he went touched Herzl to his depths. They took him to their anxious hearts as a saviour. He went from Russia straight to the Sixth Zionist Congress at Basle, fiercely determined to persuade the delegates to do something without delay to alleviate the tragedy of East European Jewry. They must adopt the Uganda scheme until some progress was made on Palestine.

CHAPTER THIRTEEN

The Passing of Herzl

THE Sixth Zionist Congress at Basle in August, 1903, was hostile to Herzl. In the months that had passed many elements had combined to stimulate opposition to him and his policies. One of these was the publication of his novel 'Altneuland'. He had planned this romance just before he had become completely engrossed in writing 'Judenstaat'. Now at last the work, completed despite all his heavy commitments, was published in the late autumn of 1902. The book told of a man who arrived in the new Judea in 1924 and saw all that had taken shape there: the farms, the industries, the irrigation, the schools; everything that makes a modern thriving nation.

The book inspired many by its power, its faith and its vision. But many others, especially Ahad Haam and other veteran East European Zionists, were deeply angered. They said this was further proof that Herzl was far too concerned with political machinations and persisted in neglecting the living culture of Jewry. They claimed that he underestimated the need to go out into the world and revive the Jewish spirit, and so bring up a new generation of young Jews who would be attached to the Zionist cause by profound moral conviction.

Before the plenary session of the Sixth Congress opened, and after he had attended worship in the Great Synagogue of Basle, Herzl met the Greater Actions Committee, and laid the Uganda offer before them. Some stared at him in shocked surprise. This confirmed all their fears. Here was a man so completely immersed in political and diplomatic action that he had forgotten Zion and was prepared to trade the ancestral soil of Palestine for Africa. Others, like the delegate from Kishinev itself, said that in their opinion the Jews would go through hell to escape from Russia.

Herzl, whose heart was troubling him greatly, took no part in the angry discussion that followed. After a bitter and heated debate it was resolved to lay the matter before a full session of Congress. The whole body would decide whether to proceed with Uganda. Herzl devoted himself to preparing his opening speech. He formulated an offer to resign if by stepping down he could save the unity of the Zionist movement.

He spoke to the opening session. The news that he had actually secured from the rulers of the British Empire, then at the height of its power and prestige, the firm offer of a territory in which Jews would have a Jewish governor and enjoy a large measure of autonomy, made delegates feel that the wings of Messianic deliverance were beating very close.

He was careful to point out that the acceptance of Uganda could never be a substitute for Zion.

'Zion? No! This is not and never will be Zion. This settlement will be a small, partial means of rescue. The new factor it represents is that it offers elements of sovereignty. It will not be the signal for the mass exodus of our people. It is only a partial rescue operation.'

He went on to emphasise that the promise of support he had extracted from the Tsar's advisers during his stay in Russia gave an important political impetus to their movement.

In the general debate that followed opposition developed. Strangely enough, it was led by those whom Herzl had mainly intended to help through the Uganda proposal. The greatest sufferers from persecution were the Russian Zionists. Now it was they who most vehemently declared that for them Zionism meant the soil of Palestine–Zion or nothing. The movement had no right to deviate from the straight road that led to Zion. They had suffered during nearly two thousand years of exile; they could suffer a generation longer; but Palestine it had to be.

There was a dramatic moment when a young girl ran through the hall, mounted the platform and, sobbing bitterly, tore down the map of Uganda that had been substituted for that of Palestine on the wall behind the dais. Herzl took little part in these debates. He was too ill. His mother was present at the Congress. At one moment, overcome by the way things were going and the pain in his heart that seemed to spell his end, he threw himself into her arms and sobbed like a child.

Eventually a compromise resolution on Uganda was put before Congress. It was decided by 295 votes to 177 to send an expedition to Africa to survey and to investigate the area. The Russian delegates, deeply outraged when Herzl criticised their opposition, left the hall in a body. It took almost the last reserves of his failing strength and all his faith and diplomacy to bring them back to the meetings. As he entered the room to speak to them he heard a voice hiss, 'Traitor!' The others were stonily silent. It was his offer to resign there and then if they really thought he had betrayed Zion which brought them back.

The discord over the Uganda issue and other problems continued to the end of the Congress. As Herzl addressed the final session, the last impression delegates had of their leader was of a man whose tall, erect body was beginning to bend in a brief surrender to pain and sickness. His face was drawn with emotion, but his eyes blazed with faith as he passionately proclaimed: 'If I forget thee, O Jerusalem, let my right hand forget its cunning.'

After the delegates had dispersed Herzl did not spare himself. He asked his colleagues in London to press for the Uganda offer to be put into definite terms. He wrote to Plehve in St. Petersburg, giving him an account of the Congress and expressing his astonishment at the way the Russian delegates had opposed the Uganda project. He used this fact as an argument to persuade the Russian statesman that only Palestine could draw off appreciable numbers of Jews from the Tsar's dominions. He said that the collapse of Zionism would strengthen the revolutionary forces in Russia. So he asked Plehve to support him in his further endeavours to get Jews the right to settle in Palestine as their national home on a basis in harmony with the aims of Zionism.

This was only one aspect of a last burst of diplomatic activity in which Herzl appealed passionately to all his old friends and contacts among the rulers and statesmen of Europe for help to obtain Palestine.

His anxiety to revive hopes of getting some part of Palestine was increased by the fact that Britain was now cooling off on the Uganda project. The British settlers there were not prepared to accept a Jewish colony, and the existence of a considerable opposition to the scheme in the Zionist Congress made Britain doubtful about its success.

He also tried to revive the El Arish plan, but met with no response from either the influential Jews of England or the British authorities whose support was essential for a further approach to Egypt.

But the most formidable opposition to all he was trying to do suddenly developed inside the Zionist movement. Menahem Ussishkin, who later became President of the Jewish National Fund, was one of the most powerful leaders of the Russian Zionists.

At the time of the Sixth Congress he was in Palestine organising the Jewish community there for Zionism. Now he made it quite clear that the Palestinian Jews would condemn the Uganda project outright. When he returned to Europe in the autumn of 1903 he organised the Russian Zionists against Herzl. A proposal was mooted, and seriously considered, to form a breakaway Congress of Russian Zionists which would concentrate on Palestine to the exclusion of all else. These elements met at Kharkov that winter and decided to oppose the Uganda scheme and to send a delegation to Herzl in Vienna.

At the beginning of 1904 a certain Papal Count, Lippay, a converted Jew, arranged for Herzl to be received in audience by the Pope. Lippay hoped that Herzl might be converted to Christianity as the price for Papal support of the Zionist movement. But the Pope, as head of the Roman Catholic Church, felt unable to agree to recommend the Zionist scheme for Palestine. Herzl had himself caused some offence by neglecting to kiss the Pope's hand, as was the custom. The audience ended with neither party convinced.

Meanwhile, a battle had begun inside the World Zionist Organisation for the unity of the movement. Herzl published a full account of the Kharkov meeting in 'Die Welt' and Jewry sided with him in an outburst of passionate devotion. Britain was still keeping the door ajar in East Africa. This proved embarrassing to Herzl. He had one last wish – to leave the Zionist Organisation united. He felt that his days were numbered. He decided he would either fight the opposition to a standstill or reconcile them to remaining within the organisation. On April 11, 1904, he addressed a meeting of the Great Actions Committee in Vienna.

He told them he was anxious only for peace. He was prepared to forget all recriminations and unhappy language, in so far as they affected him personally. However, he insisted that the unity of the Zionist Organisation must be restored.

As the meetings continued the delegates were deeply moved by the desperate sincerity with which this mortally sick leader affirmed his faith in Zionism and his belief that it had to be realised in Zion. And yet he moved them also by his passionate concern to bring the hope of a temporary refuge to the suffering Jews of Eastern Europe.

He succeeded in drawing the fragments of the World Zionist Organisation together into an enduring unity. It now remained to find the money to finance the Uganda expedition. Through his friend, Lord Rothschild, he tried to make contact with Jacob Schiff, who was then in Europe. The latter was perhaps the most noted Jewish banker and philanthropist in the U.S.A., and his benefactions were both princely and constructive. However, he was not a Zionist, as Herzl understood the word. He said once that 'the Jewish problem in Russia must be solved by and in Russia.' Nevertheless, he sought to use the influence of his and other banks to press the Russian Government to improve the position of the

Jews. One of Herzl's last acts was to send Schiff a report in which he stressed that money widely scattered on a number of projects to alleviate Jewish suffering was likely to be wasted.

All this was the last flickering of an exhausted body. On May 1, he felt so ill that he had to submit to his physicians. They ordered him to take six months' complete rest.

He did not accept the verdict graciously. The next day he spent trying to clear up his correspondence. He had to go for his rest cure, but he continued to write letters. He told his faithful David Wolffsohn not to let his mother know how ill he was.

'And don't you do anything silly when I'm no longer here,' he added gently.

He wrote again to Plehve in St. Petersburg. At the head of the draft of his letter he painfully scrawled in English the words, 'Broken down'.

He was visited by Dr. N. Katzenelsohn, a Zionist leader. He told him: 'The bell has tolled for me. I am not afraid. I can face death calmly. The last few years of my life have not been useless. I served my people faithfully.'

He did not improve at Franzensbad, so he went back to Vienna. On June 3, he decided to visit his favourite summer resort at Edlach with his wife, Julie. His heart condition was now complicated by bronchial catarrh which gradually worsened to pneumonia. A nurse was summoned to attend him, but Julie gave her little chance. As long as she could stand on her feet she did not leave Theodor's side.

Only now, as her husband lay on his death bed, was she able to have him completely to herself after the years when his dedication to Zionism had so often taken him away from her and their children.

His condition deteriorated throughout that month; it was clear that the end was not far off. Four of his closest friends came to be with him. His daughter, Pauline, was at his side. To one of his associates he said: 'I always believed I knew what real fear meant. But all that I could imagine pales into insignificance before this dreadful present horror.'

He gasped painfully. 'You see. I cannot breathe. Not to be able to breathe, that is horrible. Horrible. Oh to be able to breathe freely.'

He coughed and saw that he had brought up some blood. His sense of humour had not deserted him. 'I never thought I'd shed my blood this way,' he said. He turned to Reich, the secretary of the Congress Bureau. 'You will soon have to call Congress together,' he exclaimed. He pointed in semi-delirium to different places on the bedspread, which he must have thought was a map. 'You will buy land, here . . . here . . . and here,' he ordered.

On Friday, July 1, he felt that he was sinking. He asked for his children, Hans and Trude, to be summoned. His old friend Hechler came to see him.

'Give my greetings to the land of Israel,' he told him. 'I have given my life's blood for my people.'

He turned to his doctors and implored them: 'Keep me alive till my mother comes.'

Pointing to the guard of honour of student Zionists

who had come from Vienna, he said, 'These young men shall see the Jewish State.'

At noon on Sunday his mother arrived. When she came into the room, he tried to raise himself into a half-sitting position.

'Mother dear,' he smiled at her, 'it is so good to have you with me. You look well. I don't. But I shall soon be much better.'

With a breaking heart Jeannette Herzl looked down at her son. She saw the finely moulded, handsome features yellow with fever and drawn with pain. His brow was beaded with sweat. His breath came heavily and with an ominous whistling. The hands, once so strong and resolute, moved feebly and restlessly over the counterpane.

He tried to pretend to his younger children. They had not been told he was ill. He had forbidden it. He was ill so often that he did not want them to suffer the insecurity of feeling they had an invalid father. He was almost gay as they bent down to kiss him tenderly and as he kissed them back.

His strength was leaving him now; he was becoming delirious. By the words he said he evidently thought he was presiding over some meeting. Then he rested and seemed to sleep. Those present left the room, leaving his faithful associate, Dr. Sigmund Werner, who then edited 'Die Welt', to attend to him. At 5 p.m. Werner turned aside to prepare a hypodermic injection. He heard a deep sigh. He swung round. Herzl's head had fallen sideways on his pillow. He was dead.

Dr. Werner called in the attendant physicians. There was nothing they could do. They left the room. He gently closed his patient's eyes, went out into the garden, and wept.

Herzl's body was taken to Vienna and, as he had ordered in his will, it was prepared for burial according to the strictest Orthodox Jewish rites. His bier rested for a while in an empty room in his home. There, apart from the candles that burned at the head and foot, the only objects were a casket containing a Scroll of the Law, given to Herzl by the Jews of Vilna, and a Menorah or eight-branched candlestick.

Notables in over 500 carriages and thousands of weeping Jews on foot followed his coffin through the streets of Vienna to the Doeblinger cemetery. He was buried beside his father. In the last years of his life he had desperately fought off every attack of illness in the hope that he would live long enough to be buried in the Jewish State. In that hope he lived and in that hope he died. In the tomb he lay and waited.

CHAPTER FOURTEEN

Forty-five Years Later

IT was a clear, bright sunny day on August 16, 1949, forty-five years after the interment in the Doeblinger cemetery, when an aeroplane, with blue and white markings and the insignia of the State of Israel, landed at Lydda Airport. On board was a guard of honour of soldiers of the Israeli Army. The aircraft brought the remains of Theodor Herzl for interment in the Jewish State, as he had asked in his will.

All that day the coffin lay in state in the first all-Jewish city, Tel Aviv. The site chosen was a square before the building which temporarily housed Israel's Knesset or parliament.

There the Prime Minister, Mr. David Ben-Gurion, spoke to the nation.

'There are only two great Jews whose bones have been brought here by the people – Joseph, the son of Jacob the Patriarch, and now Benjamin [the Hebrew for Theodor], also the son of Jacob.

'Even Moses was not permitted by the Almighty

to experience what we propose to do with Herzl this day.'

From the Knesset the body was taken on the long, slow, winding route upwards to Jerusalem. The way was lined with Jews from all countries of the world, who paid grateful tribute to the passing cortège. Jews from Eastern Europe mingled with those from the free and prosperous Western lands. All were citizens of the new Israel. By the wayside stood newly arrived citizens from Rumania, the grandchildren of those who, fleeing from their persecutors nearly fifty years before, had aroused such compassion in Herzl's heart. These had a State which welcomed them. There were Jews who had survived the Nazi death-camps. Among the six million who perished was one middle-aged woman who took with her to Theresienstadt, where she died in 1943, the letters which her father, Theodor, and her mother, Julie, had exchanged. She was Trude, Theodor Herzl's younger daughter. Most of those whom death spared had languished for three years after the Second World War in displaced persons' camps throughout Europe until the establishment of the Jewish State in May, 1948, had miraculously given them a home.

There were children in whose eyes wonder struggled with tears. They had known almost nothing of love, or laughter, or happiness, until the Jewish State planned by Herzl had arisen and summoned them to a new life bright with joy and freedom, love and a new home.

There were turbaned Jews from ancient India, sidelocked Jews from the forgotten highland desert of the Yemen, Jews from Africa and Asia. They had come to the homeland from every clime, every level of civilisation, every degree of persecution and freedom. They stood in silence and watched as the man who had made their new life possible passed to his rest on the holy mountains of Zion.

At last he came to a bare windswept hill, the highest point in Jerusalem. Beside his abiding place, renamed Mount Herzl, a portion of land had been set aside for the slain warriors of Israel, the young men and women who gave their lives for their people. Here Herzl was laid to rest while the nation's leaders and the people paid him homage.

There at last the great heart lies at peace. There every year on the eve of the anniversary of Israel's independence the nation gathers to celebrate its newly won liberty. There every year a guard of honour of the élite of Israel's forces stands round the grave while new immigrants come and light torches. Every time the Greater Actions Committee or Congress meets in Jerusalem it comes to Herzl and pays him the tribute of its re-dedication to the purposes he called into being. The children of Jerusalem go on pilgrimage to this spot and are solemn as long as children can be, and then begin to laugh and play, intoxicated by the fresh wind that always sings over the unfenced grave, and by the breadth of the view from the mountain top, which takes in the vast sweep over the embracing Judean hills.

There the body of Herzl sleeps for ever, but perchance, as the native children of Israel romp happily in Zion, he too rejoices in their happiness.